The Economics of
Macro Issues

The Pearson Series in Economics

* denotes MyEconLab titles. Log onto **www.myeconlab.com** to learn more.

The Economics of
Macro Issues

FIFTH EDITION

Roger LeRoy Miller
Research Professor of Economics
University of Texas-Arlington

Daniel K. Benjamin
Clemson University, South Carolina
and PERC, Bozeman, Montana

Boston Columbus Indianapolis New York San Francisco Upper Saddle River
Amsterdam Cape Town Dubai London Madrid Milan Munich Paris Montreal Toronto
Delhi Mexico City Sao Paulo Sydney Hong Kong Seoul Singapore Taipei Tokyo

Editorial Director: Sally Yagan
Editor in Chief: Donna Battista
Acquisitions Editor: Noel Kamm Seibert
Editorial Project Manager: Carolyn Terbush
Managing Editor: Nancy H. Fenton
Senior Production Supervisor: Kathryn Dinovo
Project Manager: Pat Brown
Operations Specialist: Pat Brown
Executive Marketing Manager: Lori DeShazo
Marketing Assistant: Kim Lovato
Permissions Project Manager: Michael Joyce

Senior Manufacturing Buyer: Carol Melville
Creative Art Director: Jayne Conte
Manager, Visual Research and
  Permissions: Karen Sanatar
Cover Designer: Jon Boylan
Text Designer: Central Publishing
Production Coordination: Pat Brown
Full Service Project Management: Element LLC
Composition: Central Publishing
Printer/Binder: Interior, Edwards Brothers;
Cover, Lehigh-Phoenix Color/Hagerstown

Library of Congress Cataloging-in-Publication Data
Miller, Roger LeRoy.
  The economics of macro issues / Roger LeRoy Miller, Daniel K. Benjamin. — 5th ed.
    p. cm.
  Includes bibliographical references and index.
  ISBN-13: 978-0-321-71679-8 (pbk. : alk. paper)
  ISBN-10: 0-321-71679-5 (alk. paper)
  1. Macroeconomics.   I. Benjamin, Daniel K.   II. Title.
HB172.5.M53 2012
339—dc22   2011011873

10 9 8 7 6 5 4 3 2 1

ISBN-10: 0-321-71679-5
ISBN-13: 978-0-321-71679-8

To Marilyn and Tullio,
Thanks for your support and your advice.
—R.L.M.

To my students over the years,
With gratitude for all they have taught me.
—D.K.B.

BRIEF CONTENTS

Suggestions for Use

At the request of our readers, we include the following table to help you incorporate the chapters of this book into your syllabus. Depending on the breadth of your course, you may also want to consult the companion paperback, *The Economics of Public Issues,* 17th edition, which features microeconomics topics and a similar table in its preface.

Economics Topics	Recommended Chapters in The Economics of Macro Issues, 5th Edition
Taxes and Public Spending	2, 13, 14, 16, 17, 18, 19
Unemployment, Inflation, and Deflation	8, 9, 11, 12, 20, 21
Measuring the Economy's Performance	2, 6, 12
Economic Growth and Development	1, 2, 3, 4, 5, 10, 13
Classical and Keynesian Macro Analyses	6, 8, 9, 13, 14, 18
Fiscal Policy	13, 14, 15, 16, 17, 18, 19
Deficits and the Public Debt	13, 14, 15, 16, 17, 18, 19
Money and Banking	11, 22, 23
Money Creation and Deposit Insurance	15, 20, 21, 22, 23
Monetary Policy: Domestic and International	20, 21, 24, 27
Stabilization and the Global Economy	24, 26
International Trade	1, 3, 24, 25, 26
International Finance	27
Recession	7, 8, 9, 13

PREFACE

Times have changed, and so has this book. Once again, the macro-economic policy scene has witnessed a profound transformation over a remarkably short period of time. Since our last revision, the United States has endured one of the most severe recessions of the past hundred years, and both fiscal and monetary policy have changed dramatically. Indeed, agencies of the U.S. government—ranging from the Treasury to government-sponsored enterprises—have become the *de facto* guarantors of most of the U.S. housing market and virtually every large-scale commercial venture in the nation. The Federal Reserve System has expanded its credit allocation operations to make itself into an industrial policy fiefdom. And along the way, the U.S. taxpayer has been put on the hook, explicitly or implicitly, for trillions of dollars in new obligations. Not since World War II has the American economy undergone such change.

POLICY REVOLUTION

In short, things have happened to the economy that many economists had thought impossible, and the fiscal and monetary authorities have responded with nothing short of revolutionary changes in the way they conduct policy. Because this book is about our times, these changes have induced us to once again transform this edition of *The Economics of Macro Issues*. As just one example, virtually the entire section dealing with fiscal policy has been thrown out, and we have started again from scratch. The result of our revisions, we believe, is a book that addresses more critical new issues with more timeliness and, we hope, more insight than any prior edition. We also believe that we are able to showcase pivotal developments in economic affairs and policymaking in ways that no other book on the market can match.

NEW TO THIS EDITION

The new issues addressed in this edition include the following:

- Going Underground—how the underground economy sustains prosperity
- The Threat to Growth—why higher taxes can mean less prosperity
- Is GDP What We Want?—is there a better measure than GDP?
- The Great Recession—why it happened and why it was a big deal

- Are You Stimulated Yet?—why stimulus packages do—or don't—work
- Health Care Reform—why spending more will get you less
- The Fannie Mae, Freddie Mac Flimflam—your money at waste
- Big Bucks for Bailouts—if it's "too big to fail," it's too big to save
- The Pension Crisis—the future is coming and it's going to crush us
- The Fed Feeding Frenzy—why monetary policy no longer looks like it used to

In addition to completely replacing more than one-third of the book, all of the remaining chapters have been touched in one way or another by the revision. Moreover, we have roughly doubled the number of questions appearing at the end of each chapter, and done so in a way that will provide both challenge and enlightenment to students at all levels of academic achievement. Quite simply, we have sought to provide a book that reflects in every dimension the major transformations that have taken place in the American economy over the past few years, and to ensure accessibility of the results to all. The result, we believe, will stimulate readers in unprecedented ways.

INSTRUCTOR'S MANUAL

Every instructor will want to access the *Instructor's Manual* that accompanies *The Economics of Macro Issues*. It is available online to all adopters of the book. For each chapter, the manual provides the following:

- A synopsis that cuts to the core of the economic issues involved in the chapter.
- A concise exposition of the "behind-the-scenes" economic analysis on which the discussion in the text is based. In almost all cases, this exposition is supplemented with one or more diagrams that we have found to be particularly useful as teaching tools.
- Answers to the Discussion Questions posed at the end of the chapter—answers that further develop the basic economic analysis of the chapter and almost always suggest new avenues of discussion.

THE REVIEW TEAM

Of course, an undertaking such as this revision requires an enormous amount of behind-the-scenes activity, and we have been fortunate to have some of the best helpmates imaginable. The following individuals contributed considerably to this revision, offering key proposals for new topics and approaches and often e-mailing us with suggestions even as the revision was taking place. They played an integral role in our efforts.

Thomas Birch, University of New Hampshire-Manchester
Kent M. Ford, SUNY Onondaga Community College
John Krieg, Western Washington University
Ihsuan Li, Minnesota State University
Cyril Morong, San Antonio College
Randall Russell, Yavapai College

To all of these individuals, we offer our most sincere thanks. Although we were unable to do everything they wanted, we believe that each of them will be able to see the impact they had on the book.

The Production Team

Our thanks also go to the individuals involved in the hands-on production process. As usual, Sue Jasin of K&M Consulting contributed expert typing and editing and Robbie Benjamin was unstinting in her demands for clarity of thought and exposition. We also thank our editors at Pearson, Noel Seibert, Carolyn Terbush, and Kathryn Dinovo, for their encouragement and help in this project.

R.L.M.
D.K.B.

PART ONE

The Miracle of Economic Growth

CHAPTER 1

Rich Nation, Poor Nation

Why do the citizens of some nations grow rich while the inhabitants of others remain poor? Your initial answer might be "because of differences in the **natural-resource endowments** of the nations." It is true that ample endowments of energy, timber, and fertile land all help increase **wealth.** But natural resources can be only a very small part of the answer, as witnessed by many counterexamples. Switzerland and Luxembourg, for example, are nearly devoid of key natural resources, and yet decade after decade, the real income of citizens of those lands has grown rapidly, propelling them to great prosperity. Similarly, Hong Kong, which consists of but a few square miles of rock and hillside, is one of the economic miracles of modern times, while in Russia, a land amply endowed with vast quantities of virtually every important resource, most people remain mired in economic misery.

UNRAVELING THE MYSTERY OF GROWTH

A number of recent studies have begun to unravel the mystery of **economic growth.** Repeatedly, they have found that it is the fundamental political and legal **institutions** of society that are conducive to growth. Of these, political stability, secure private property rights, and legal systems based on the **rule of law** are among the most important. Such institutions encourage people to make long-term investments in improvements to land and in all forms of **physical** and **human capital.** These investments raise the **capital stock,** which in turn provides for more growth long into the future. And the cumulative effects of this growth over time eventually yield much higher **standards of living.**

Table 1–1 Differing Legal Systems

Common Law Nations	Civil Law Nations
Australia	Brazil
Canada	Egypt
India	France
Israel	Greece
New Zealand	Italy
United Kingdom	Mexico
United States	Sweden

Professor Paul Mahoney of the University of Virginia, for example, has studied the contrasting effects of different legal systems on economic growth. Many legal systems around the world today are based on one of two models: the English **common law system** and the French **civil law system.** Common law systems reflect a conscious decision in favor of a limited role for government and emphasize the importance of the judiciary in constraining the power of the executive and legislative branches of government. In contrast, civil law systems favor the creation of a strong centralized government in which the legislature and the executive branch have the power to grant preferential treatment to special interests. Table 1-1 shows a sample of common law and civil law nations.

THE IMPORTANCE OF SECURE PROPERTY RIGHTS

Mahoney finds that the security of property rights is much stronger in nations with common law systems, such as the United Kingdom and its former colonies, including the United States. In nations such as France and its former colonies, the civil law systems are much more likely to yield unpredictable changes in the rules of the game—the structure of **property and contract rights.** This, in turn, makes people reluctant to make long-term fixed investments in nations with civil law systems, a fact that ultimately slows their growth and lowers the standard of living of their citizens.

The reasoning is simple. If the police will not help you protect your rights to a home or car, you are less likely to acquire those **assets.** Similarly, if you cannot easily enforce business or employment contracts, you are much less likely to enter into those contracts—and thus less likely to produce as many goods or services. Furthermore, if you cannot plan for the future because you don't know what the rules of the game will be ten years or perhaps even one year from now, you are far less likely to make productive long-term investments that require years to pay off. Common law systems seem to do a better job at enforcing contracts and securing property rights and thus would be expected to promote economic activity now and economic growth over time.

When Mahoney examined the economic performance of nations around the world from 1960 until the 1990s, he found that economic growth has been one-third higher in the common law nations, with their strong property rights, than it has been in civil law nations. Over the years covered by his study, the increase in the standard of living—measured by **real per capita income**—was more than 20 percent greater in common law nations than in civil law nations. If such a pattern persisted over the span of a century, it would produce a staggering 80 percent differential in terms of real per capita income in favor of nations with secure property rights.

THE IMPORTANCE OF OTHER INSTITUTIONS

The economists William Easterly and Ross Levine have taken a much broader view, both across time and across institutions, assessing the economic growth of a variety of nations since their days as colonies. These authors examine how institutions such as political stability, protection of persons and property against violence or theft, security of contracts, and freedom from regulatory burdens contribute to sustained economic growth. They find that it is key institutions such as these, rather than natural-resource endowments, that explain long-term differences in growth and thus present-day differences in levels of real income. To illustrate the powerful effect of institutions, consider the contrast between Mexico, with a real per capita income of about $14,000 today, and the United States, with a real per capita income of about $50,000. Easterly and Levine conclude that if Mexico had developed with the same political and legal institutions that the United States has enjoyed, per capita income in Mexico today would be equal to that in the United States.

THE HISTORICAL ROOTS OF TODAY'S INSTITUTIONS

In light of the tremendous importance of institutions in determining long-term growth, Easterly and Levine go on to ask another important question: How have countries gotten the political and legal institutions they have today? The answer has to do with disease, of all things. The seventy-two countries Easterly and Levine examined are all former European colonies in which a variety of colonial strategies were pursued. In Australia, New Zealand, and North America, the colonists found geography and climate that were conducive to good health. Permanent settlement in such locations was attractive, and so the settlers created institutions to protect private property and curb the power of the state. But when Europeans arrived in Africa and South America, they encountered tropical diseases—such as malaria and yellow fever—that produced high mortality among the settlers. This discouraged permanent settlement and encouraged a mentality focused on extracting metals, cash crops, and other resources. This, in turn, provided little incentive to promote democratic institutions or stable long-term property rights systems. The differing initial institutions helped shape economic growth over the years, and their persistence continues to shape the political and legal character and the standard of living in these nations today.

NO PROPERTY RIGHTS, NO PROPERTY

Recent events also illustrate that the effects of political and legal institutions can be drastically accelerated—at least in the wrong direction. When Zimbabwe won its independence from Great Britain in 1980, it was one of the most prosperous nations in Africa. Soon after taking power as Zimbabwe's first (and thus far only) president, Robert Mugabe began disassembling that nation's rule of law, tearing apart the institutions that had helped it grow rich. He reduced the security of property rights in land and eventually confiscated those rights altogether. Mugabe has also gradually taken control of the prices of most goods and services in his nation. The Mugabe government has even confiscated large **stocks** of food and most other things of value that might be exported out of or imported into Zimbabwe. In short, anything that is produced or saved has become subject to confiscation, so the incentives to do either are—to put it mildly—reduced. As a result, between 1980 and 1996, real per capita income in Zimbabwe fell by one-third, and since 1996 it has fallen by an additional third. Eighty percent of the workforce is unemployed, investment is nonexistent, and the annual inflation rate reached *231 million percent* in 2008—just before the monetary system collapsed completely. Decades of labor and capital investment have been destroyed because the very institutions that made progress possible have been eliminated. It is a lesson we ignore at our peril.

FOR CRITICAL ANALYSIS

1. Consider two countries, A and B, and suppose that both have identical *physical* endowments of, say, iron ore. But in country A, any profits that are made from mining the ore are subject to

confiscation by the government, while in country B, there is no such risk. How does the risk of expropriation affect the *economic endowments* of the two nations? In which nation are people richer?

2. In light of your answer to question 1, how do you explain the fact that in some countries there is widespread political support for government policies that expropriate resources from some groups for the purpose of handing them out to other groups?

3. Going to college in the United States raises average lifetime earnings by about two-thirds, given our current political and economic institutions. But suppose that ownership of the added income generated by your college education suddenly became uncertain. Specifically, suppose a law was passed in your state that enabled the governor to select 10 percent of the graduating class from all of the state's colleges and universities each year and impose a tax of up to 50 percent on the difference between the earnings of these people in their first job and the average earnings of people in the state who have only a high school education. What would happen to immigration into or out of the state? What would happen to attendance at colleges and universities within the state? If the governor were allowed to arbitrarily decide who got hit with the new tax, what would happen to campaign contributions to the governor? What would happen to the number of people "volunteering" to work in the governor's next campaign? Would your decision to invest in a college education change? Explain your responses.

4. Go to a source such as the CIA factbook or the World Bank and collect per capita income and population data for each of the nations listed in Table 1-1. Compare the average per capita income of the common law with the average per capita income of the civil law countries. Based on the discussion in the chapter, identify at least two other factors that you think are important to take into account when assessing whether the differences you observe are likely due to the systems of the countries.

5. Most international attempts to aid people living in low-income nations have come in one of two forms: (i) gifts of consumer goods (such as food), and (ii) assistance in constructing or obtaining capital goods (such as tractors or dams or roads). Based on what you have learned in this chapter, how likely are such efforts to *permanently* raise the standard of living in such countries? Explain.

6. Louisiana and Quebec both have systems of local law (state and provincial, respectively) that are heavily influenced by their common French heritage, which includes civil law. What do you predict is true about per capita income in Louisiana compared to the other U.S. states, and per capita income in Quebec, compared to the other Canadian provinces? Is this prediction confirmed by the facts (which can be readily ascertained with a few quick Web searches)? Identify at least two other factors that you think are important to take into account when assessing whether the differences you observe are likely due to the influence of civil law institutions.

CHAPTER 2

Going Underground

Consider the following types of workers:

- "Gypsy" taxi drivers in some U.S. cities
- Rickshaw drivers in Kolkata, India
- Street vendors in Kiev, Ukraine
- Sidewalk tortilla sellers in Mexico City, Mexico

While these people speak different languages, use different currencies, and have different skill levels, they all have one thing in common—they are part of the **underground economy.** They deal in cash only and usually pay no taxes, regardless of their earnings. They all work "off the books." There are no official statistics about them, only rough estimates provided by the International Labour Organization (ILO), a few government agencies, and economists interested in this topic.

Before we examine data concerning the size of the underground economy, let's first examine why anyone would want to participate in this "shadow," or "informal," economy.

THE ECONOMICS OF ACTIVITY THAT IS ILLEGAL

Certainly, if you are engaged in the illegal drug trade anywhere in the world, you cannot be part of the **official, reported economy.** You have to use cash and also be careful that your illegal transactions cannot be traced by government authorities, including tax collectors. Otherwise, you'll soon be headed for jail.

Of course, there is no way to know exactly how much underground activity is centered in the illegal drug trade. Estimates of the worldwide total vary from $300 billion per year to well over $1 trillion per year. While the U.S. $100 dollar bill used to be the drug dealers' cash of choice, now they often use 500-euro notes (worth about $700). Consider that a $1 million in $100 bills weighs 22 pounds—which would fill a very heavy carryon that might be searched. The same amount in 500-euro bills weighs just 3.2 pounds. The increased use of euro bills for illegal transactions has benefited the **European Central Bank (ECB)** because it costs very little to produce euro currency compared to that currency's **face value.**

Not all illegal activities involve drugs, to be sure. The purchase and sale of human organs, for example, is part of the underground economy around the world. Paying for someone else's kidney in the United States is an illegal activity, as it is in most countries. Nevertheless, some of those who are on the waiting list for kidney transplants sometimes turn to "matchmakers" who will find a perfectly healthy person who is willing to donate an organ—for a price. And the price for the organ—usually acquired from a donor who lives in another country—will likely range from $5,000 to $25,000 (and up). All in cash, all unreported, and all part of the underground economy.

TAXES DO MAKE A DIFFERENCE

Despite drugs and human organs, however, the most important stimulus for the underground economy likely comes from taxes. Let's face it, if your **marginal tax rate** were only, say, 15 percent, how much effort would you spend to avoid reporting income? Probably not very much, given that each dollar of unreported income would only save you 15 cents in taxes. In contrast, at a marginal income tax rate of, say, 40 percent, you might be tempted to seek plenty of ways to earn unreported income. In other words, you might wish to become part of the underground economy, at least for some portion of your annual income.

We thus infer that in every country in the world, the greater the marginal income tax rate, the larger will be the share of total annual economic activity that will be unreported and therefore untaxed. This conclusion merely reflects the fact that everyone responds to incentives on the **margin.** Now, this does not mean that high marginal tax rates cause the entire workforce to seek off-the-books income. Rather, the higher the marginal income tax rates are, the greater will be the proportion of individuals who will seek to earn unreported income.

A comparison of Europe and the United States suggests that our conclusion about the importance of taxes is correct. European nations, on average, have imposed higher marginal tax rates on their citizens than has the United States. Estimates of the size of the underground economy are that it is twice as large in Europe as a share of the economy as it is in the United States. About 10 percent of total economic activity in the United States appears to be underground, but the number is over 20 percent for Europe. There is one thing we can be confident of for the United States. If marginal income tax rates rise compared to what they were during the period 2003–2010, the relative size of the underground economy will grow. This is just one reason why, when government officials make their calculations of increased tax revenues due to new higher tax rates, they are consistently wrong. The officials fail to take into account the movement into the underground economy that is induced by higher marginal tax rates, and thus overestimate the amount of increased tax revenues from the higher rates.

The Impact of Labor Market Regulations

In many European countries, particularly France, Germany, and Italy, firing a poorly performing worker is extremely difficult, and in some cases impossible. The amount of paperwork and legal proceedings that an employer has to undertake to get rid of a worker is sometimes beyond belief—at least for Americans. There is even a special judicial system in France for people who are fired. Employers lose the legal battles more than 75 percent of the time.

How do employers react to such an environment? Some, particularly smaller businesses, seek out workers who agree to cash payments and no employment contracts. Thus, workers may face the option of accepting a cash-only job with no job security instead of becoming or remaining unemployed. Moreover, in all countries in which **unemployment benefits** last for many months or even many years, the unemployed are more willing to participate in the underground economy because they if they work "off the books" for cash, they can continue to receive unemployment benefits.

In 2010 the U.S. Congress increased the length of eligibility for unemployment benefits to almost two years. In response, some of the people receiving those extended benefits began to seriously seek "off-the-books" jobs, just as their counterparts have long done in Europe. What is a way of life for the unemployed in France, Italy, and Spain has started to become more widespread in America.

Other recent legislation has added to the incentives to become part of the underground economy in the United States. We speak here of the federal health-care legislation passed in 2010, which will, over the next few years, create additional regulations and costs to businesses that offer health insurance to their workers. As a result, some of those businesses will only be willing to hire additional workers if those new workers remain off the books, and thus ineligible for high-cost, employer-provided health insurance. This will increase the number of people seeking government-subsidized health insurance, and thus help raise the costs of the health-care legislation far above the official estimates of those costs. (See Chapter 14 for more details.)

THE ESTIMATED SIZE OF THE UNDERGROUND ECONOMY

On a worldwide basis, about one-third of annual world income goes unreported. As noted earlier, estimates for the United States center on about 10 percent, while it is believed that around 20 percent of income in Europe is underground and thus goes unreported. Many southern European countries, such as Italy, have underground sectors that account for at least 30 percent of all economic activity.

When we consider developing countries and those with highly corrupt governments, the underground economy may be as great as 70 percent of all economic activity. As Venezuela went from a democracy to an oligarchy with massive amounts of corruption, the size of the underground economy in that country probably tripled, although there is no way to be sure of the exact number.

Wherever we look around the world, however, it appears that taxes, regulations, and government corruption all help stimulate expansion of the underground economy. This is because such obstacles to voluntary trade are more easily circumvented when work is "off the books."

A TALE OF TWO CITIES

In 1959 the completion of the St. Lawrence Seaway provided a short-cut around the port at Buffalo, New York. The city's economy began a gradual deterioration as fewer and fewer ships stopped there. The city's population declined by over 50 percent as residents sought opportunities elsewhere. Buffalo became a shell of its former self.

Now consider another city in another country that suffered a similar downturn. At the start of the 1980s, there were more than 60 textile mills in Ahmedabad, India, employing over 150,000 people. The textile workers received benefits and pension packages in addition to steady wages. Although total compensation in the mills was low relative to pay in the United States, it was above the average for India. But beginning in the middle of the 1980s, Ahmedabad saw its major factories reduce their output and finally shutter. China, Vietnam, and other developing countries could produce the same textiles at lower costs. Only ten mills survived in Ahmedabad, and more than 100,000 workers lost their textile jobs. When industrial decline hit Buffalo, the economic, geographic, and social mobility of the United States was high enough that most of the displaced workers found jobs elsewhere, often far away from Buffalo. When they departed, they left behind empty houses and a decaying urban center. In India, mobility is far less than in the United States. Hence, one might expect to find that Ahmedabad became plagued by high unemployment when the mills shuttered, perhaps even beset with civil unrest. In fact, Ahmedabad is thriving—all because of its underground economy.

Those former textile workers left their former industry, but they didn't leave town. Instead, they joined the city's underground economy. The city now has over 70,000 self-employed street vendors, almost 50,000 self-employed trash collectors and recyclers—well, you get the picture. Ahmedabad's informal economy has kept the city alive. It has prevented urban decay and high levels of unemployment. To be sure, the self-employed in this informal underground economy do not have the nicest jobs, nor are they paid wonderful salaries. The local municipal commissioner, I.P. Gautam, admits that per capita income is less than it used to be, "but you get your bread and butter." Indeed, Ahmedabad's underground economy is how that city survived the worldwide recession of 2007–2009.

LESSONS FOR THE FUTURE

The conclusion we draw from this tale of two cities is not that the people who lost jobs in Buffalo should have become self-employed street vendors. Instead, we infer that, particularly in developing countries, a thriving underground economy can help generate **wealth** that would not exist without it. Even in developed countries, more wealth is created through underground activities than would be generated in their absence.

If developed countries' governments continue to impose higher marginal personal income tax rates and more costly regulation of labor markets, the inevitable result will be that more work will be done off the books. Although not reported (or taxed), such work is nevertheless still wealth-creating. And for the people who engage in it, it beats their other options.

We are not suggesting that avoiding taxes by working in the underground economy is laudable. But consider the alternative. Without the option of the underground economy, some (perhaps many) of those workers pushed out of the formal economy would be pushed into more unemployment and even lower wages. Of course, there are disadvantages of the informal economy. Underground workers have fewer rights and almost no recourse to the courts when maltreated by employers. Moreover, they routinely have no fringe benefits and little job security. Nevertheless, regardless of the language spoken or the currency used, for many people around the globe, the underground world beats all other relevant alternatives.

FOR CRITICAL ANALYSIS

1. What is the relevance of marginal income tax rates when seeking to understand the extent of a country's underground economy?

2. How do employers respond to labor laws that make it difficult or costly to fire incompetent workers? Do such laws actually yield higher employment levels?

3. Is there a difference between becoming part of the underground economy because the activities in which you are dealing are illegal and simply trying to reduce the share of income that you pay in taxes? If so, what is that difference?

4. Why would you predict that a much larger share of total economic activity due to the underground economy will exist when a country's government is very corrupt? What type of activities would you expect would be part of the underground economy?

5. Is it possible that you might prefer to be paid "on the books," while your employer would prefer paying you "off the books?" If so, how would such a disagreement be settled between you?

6. When you voluntarily exchange your labor services with someone else who pays you "on the books," can you be made worse off compared to not working at all? What if you are paid "off the books?"

CHAPTER 3

Outsourcing and Economic Growth

One prominent business commentator keeps a "hit list" of corporations that send jobs overseas. Such actions are decidedly un-American, he opines, whenever he gets a chance to express his views against **outsourcing**. A recent Democratic presidential nominee had a name for heads of companies that outsourced telemarketing projects, customer services, and other white-collar jobs to foreign countries: He called them "Benedict Arnold CEOs."

Congress even tried to pass a bill to prevent any type of outsourcing by the Department of State and the Department of Defense. Republican representative Don Manzullo of Illinois said, "You can't just continue to outsource overseas time after time after time, lose your strategic military base, and then expect this Congress to sit back and see the jobs lost and do nothing." When an adviser to the president publicly stated that the foreign outsourcing of service jobs was not such a bad idea, numerous politicians lambasted him for even the suggestion that outsourcing could be viewed in a positive light.

WHAT IS THIS "OUTSOURCING?"

The concept of outsourcing is simple: Instead of hiring American workers at home, American corporations hire foreign workers to do the same jobs. For example, some of these foreign workers are in India and do call center work, answering technical questions for computer purchasers. Another job such workers do well (and cheaply) is software development and debugging. Because of low-cost communication, especially over the Internet, software programmers can be just about anywhere in the world and still work for U.S. corporations.

Besides the fear that outsourcing "robs Americans of jobs," it is also claimed that outsourcing reduces **economic growth** in the United States. (Presumably, that must mean that it increases economic growth in, say, India.) Because outsourcing is part and parcel of international trade in goods and services, the real question becomes: Can the United States have higher growth rates if it restricts American corporations from "sending jobs abroad?"

As we set out to answer this question, we must keep one simple fact in mind: Outsourcing is nothing more or less than the purchase of labor services from the residents of a foreign nation. When the Detroit Red Wings host the Vancouver Canucks, fans at the game are outsourcing: They are purchasing labor services from Canadians. In this sense, Canadian hockey players are no different from Indian software engineers; they are citizens of foreign nations who are competing with citizens of the United States in the supply of labor services. Just as important, outsourcing is no different from any other form of international trade.

THE LINK BETWEEN ECONOMIC GROWTH AND OUTSOURCING

International trade has been around for thousands of years. That means that the concept of outsourcing is certainly not new, even though the term seems to be. After all, the exchange of services between countries is a part of international trade. In any event, if we decide to restrict this type of international trade in services, we will be restricting international trade in general. Experts who study economic growth today have found that the openness of an economy is a key determinant of its rate of economic growth. Any restriction on outsourcing is a type of **trade barrier,** one that will reduce the benefits we obtain from international trade.

There is a clear historical link between economic growth and trade barriers. Figure 3-1 shows the relationship between the openness of an economy—fewer or more trade barriers—and the rate of economic growth. Along the horizontal axis of the graph is a trade barrier index, which for the United States is equal to 100. On the vertical axis, you see the average annual growth of **per capita income** in percentage terms.

It is evident from this graph that countries that have fewer international trade barriers have also had higher rates of economic growth. The lesson of history is quite clear: International trade increases economic growth, and growth boosts economic well-being. Government efforts to restrict outsourcing will restrict international trade, and this will make Americans poorer, not richer.

Figure 3–1 Relationship between Economic Growth and Barriers to International Trade

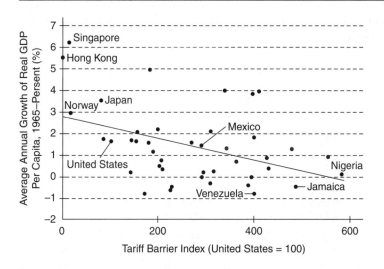

WILL THE UNITED STATES BECOME A THIRD WORLD COUNTRY?

In spite of the evidence just shown, Paul Craig Roberts, a former Reagan administration treasury official, declared at a Brookings Institution conference that "the United States will be a Third World country in twenty years." His prediction was based on the idea that entire classes of high-wage service-sector employees will eventually find themselves in competition with highly skilled workers abroad who earn much less than their U.S. counterparts. He contended that U.S. software programmers and radiologists, for example, will not be able to compete in the global economy. Thus, he argued, the United States will lose millions of white-collar jobs due to outsourcing of service-sector employment to India and China.

Jeffrey E. Garten, former dean of the Yale School of Management, reiterated and expanded on this prediction. He believes that the transfer of jobs abroad will accelerate for generations to come. He argues that in countries from China to the Czech Republic, there is a "virtually unlimited supply of industrious and educated labor working at a fraction of U.S. wages." Similarly, according to Craig Barrett, former board chair at the chipmaker Intel, American workers today face the prospect of "300 million well-educated people in India, China, and Russia who can do effectively any job that can be done" in the United States.

Still other commentators have claimed that India alone will soak up as many as four million jobs from the U.S. labor market by 2015. Some even believe that this number may exceed 10 million. If true, one might expect American software developers and call center technicians to start moving to India!

SOME OVERLOOKED FACTS

Much of the outsourcing discussion has ignored two simple facts that turn out to be important if we really want to understand what the future will bring.

1. *Outsourcing is the result of trade liberalization in foreign nations.* After decades of isolation, the markets in China, India, and Eastern Europe have begun to open up to international trade. As is often the case when governments finally allow their people to trade internationally, these governments have pushed hard to stimulate exports—of labor services as well as goods. But this cannot be a long-term equilibrium strategy because the workers producing those goods and supplying those services are doing it because they want to become consumers. Soon enough, and this is already happening, they want to spend their hard-earned income on goods and services, many of which are produced abroad. Thus, today's outsourcing of jobs to those nations must eventually turn into exports of goods and services to those same nations.

2. *Prices adjust to keep markets in balance.* The supply curve of labor is upward-sloping. Thus, as U.S. corporations hire foreign workers (either directly by outsourcing or indirectly by importing goods), market wages in foreign lands must rise. Between 2003 and 2010, for example, Indian labor-outsourcing companies saw wages rise more than 50 percent. Over a longer span, real wages in southern China (which has been open to trade far longer than India) are now *six times higher* than they were just twenty years ago. These higher wages obviously reduce the competitiveness of the firms that must pay them. Moreover, it is not just wages that adjust: The relative values of national currencies move, too. Between 2003 and 2007, the value of the dollar fell more than 25 percent, making foreign goods (and workers) more expensive here and making U.S. goods and workers more attractive in foreign markets.

Of course, adjustments are never instantaneous. Moreover, they are occurring because some American firms are moving output and employment abroad; hence, at least some U.S. workers are having to move to lower-paying jobs, often with a spell of unemployment along the way. How big is the impact in the short run, before all of the price adjustments take place? According to the Bureau of Labor Statistics, in a typical recent year, the number of jobs lost to outsourcing is measured in the thousands—out of a workforce of over 155 million. So if you are currently a U.S. software developer, you don't have to worry about packing your bags for Mumbai, at least not soon.

INSOURCING BY FOREIGN FIRMS

U.S. firms are not the only ones that engage in outsourcing. Many foreign firms do the same. When a foreign firm outsources to the United States, we can call it **insourcing**. For example, Mexican firms routinely send data to U.S. accounting businesses for calculation of payrolls and for maintaining financial records. Many foreign hospitals pay our radiologists to read X-rays and MRI images. Foreign firms use American firms to provide a host of other services, many of which involve consulting. Also, when a foreign automobile manufacturer builds an assembly plant in the United States, it is in effect outsourcing automobile assembly to American workers. Thus, American workers in the South Carolina BMW plant, the Alabama Mercedes-Benz plant, or the Toyota or Honda plants in Tennessee and Ohio are all beneficiaries of the fact that those foreign companies have outsourced jobs to the United States. Indeed, all across the country and around the world, hundreds of millions of workers are employed by "foreign" corporations—although it's becoming difficult to tell the nationality of any company, given the far-flung nature of today's global enterprises.

WHAT REALLY MATTERS: THE LONG RUN

If you own the only grocery store in your small town, you are clearly harmed if a competing store opens across the street. If you work in a small telephone equipment store and a large company starts taking away business via Internet sales, you will obviously be worse off. If you used to be employed at a call center for customer service at Wal-Mart and have just lost your job because Wal-Mart outsourced to a cheaper Indian firm, you will have to look for a new job.

These kinds of "losses" of income or jobs have occurred since the beginning of commerce. They will always exist in any dynamic economy. Indeed, if we look over the American economy as a whole, in a typical year roughly *one million workers lose their jobs every week*. But in a typical year slightly *more* than one million people find a new job every week. So on balance, employment in the United States keeps growing, even though the average person will change jobs every three years—some, no doubt, because of international competition. But job turnover like this is an essential component of a labor market that is continually adjusting to economic change. It is a sign of health, not sickness, in the economy. If you find this hard to believe, you can look west or east. In Japan, efforts to "protect" workers from international trade resulted in economic stagnation and have depressed real income growth over the past twenty years.

In Europe, similar efforts to "preserve" the jobs of existing workers have resulted in *higher*, not lower, unemployment because firms are unwilling to hire people that they cannot fire later. It is true that the pattern of job losses and gains in a given year is altered during an economic recession, such as the latest one. In particular, during the early stages of a recession, additional people lose their jobs in a given week and fewer people find a job each week, with the result being higher unemployment in the short run. But international trade is not the cause of recessions in the United States (although an economic recession can be made worse by *restrictions* on international trade, as it was in the early 1930s). On the contrary, international trade is an important source of economic prosperity.

If you are still wondering, simply look back at Figure 3–1. The lessons of history and of economics are clear: Trade creates **wealth,** and that is true whether the trade is interpersonal, interstate, or international. The reality is that labor outsourcing is simply part of a worldwide trend toward increased international trade in both goods and services. As international trade expands—assuming that politicians and bureaucrats allow it to expand—the result will be higher rates of growth and higher levels of income in America and elsewhere. American workers will continue to enjoy the fruits of that growth, just as they always have.

FOR CRITICAL ANALYSIS

1. What, if any, differences exist between competition among service workers across the fifty states and competition among service workers across nations?

2. When BMW decides to build a plant in the United States, who gains and who loses?

3. International Business Machines Corporation (IBM) recently stated that it expected to save almost $170 million annually by shifting several thousand high-paying programming jobs overseas. Explain why IBM would undertake this move. Then explain the short-run and long-run effects of this outsourcing.

4. Some companies that outsourced call centers during the 1990s have returned these centers to North America over the past decade. Who has gained and who has lost as a result of the return of the call centers to this continent? Explain.

5. The automaker BMW, whose corporate headquarters is in Germany, makes its X-series sport utility vehicles in South Carolina, and sells many of them in China. Who is outsourcing what to whom? Explain.

6. What is the difference between outsourcing and international trade?

CHAPTER 4

Poverty, Capitalism, and Growth

Fifty years ago, nearly half of the world's population lived in poverty; today, the proportion is about 17 percent. In fact, compared to fifty years ago, even though the world's population has doubled, there are actually fewer people now living below the poverty line. Despite the human misery that is evident to varying degrees in virtually every nation of the world, there is little doubt that economic prosperity has made great strides.

THE SWEEP OF HISTORY

The past half-century is but a small part of a story that has evolved over the course of 250 years or so. In the middle of the eighteenth century, perhaps 90 percent of the world's population lived in a state of **abject poverty,** subsisting on the equivalent of less than $1 per person per day, measured in today's terms. In fact, for most of human history, abject poverty—including inadequate nutrition and rudimentary shelter—was the norm for almost everyone, everywhere. This began to change in the eighteenth century with the **Industrial Revolution** and its associated mechanization of tasks that had always been laboriously done by humans or animals. Stimulated in the early years by the invention and application of the steam engine, the Industrial Revolution initiated a massive cascade of innovations in transportation, chemistry, biology, manufacturing processes, communications, and electronic technology. This continuing process of invention and innovation has made little headway in many parts of the world, but where it has taken hold, there has been a sustained rise in average **real per capita income** and a corresponding decline in poverty. By 1820, the extent of abject poverty had fallen from 90 to 80 percent; by 1900, it had dipped below 70 percent; and it has continued to decline since. Before the Industrial Revolution, more than five out of six people lived in abject poverty; today, it is one out of six.

UNEVEN PROGRESS

This story of human progress has been uneven across countries. Europe, North America, and a few other locations have witnessed the greatest increases in real per capita income and the greatest decreases in poverty. By contrast, the **standard of living** and the extent of poverty in many African nations have changed little over the past 250 years. Even within given countries, progress has sometimes been erratic. Ninety years ago, for example, the standard of living in Argentina was the sixth highest in the world; today, that nation ranks seventieth in living standards. In contrast, thirty years ago, 250 million people in China lived in abject poverty; that number has since been cut to one-tenth that number.

In Chapter 1, you saw the key institutional factors that determine average levels of **per capita income.** Secure **property and contract rights** and the **rule of law** were the **institutions** under which the Industrial Revolution flourished best, and it is thus in nations that have embraced these institutions that people are most likely to be prosperous. These same institutions are the ones typically associated with *capitalism,* economic systems that depend primarily (though not necessarily completely) on markets to allocate scarce **resources.** Of course, no country in the world is completely capitalist; in the United States, for example, less than two-thirds of resources are allocated by the private sector, while the rest are allocated by federal, state, or local governments. At the other end of the spectrum, even in Communist countries such as Cuba, Vietnam, and North Korea, markets play at least some role in allocating resources.

Despite a few ambiguities, then, it is possible to measure the degree of capitalism (or, as some would term it, economic freedom) in each country around the world. Doing so yields measures that seem to correspond reasonably well with what many people would think is true about the economies of those countries. For example, using the measures constructed by Canada's Fraser Institute, Hong Kong's economy is rated the most capitalist, while the United States is sixth. Singapore, Switzerland, New Zealand, Canada, the United Kingdom, and Australia are other nations whose economies are judged among the ten most capitalist in the world. If you know much about economic prosperity around the world, you will be aware that these countries are also among the world leaders in real per capita income. Indeed, the association of capitalism with prosperity is everywhere quite strong.

CAPITALISM AND PROSPERITY

It is convenient for our purposes to divide all the nations in the world into five groups, ranging from "most capitalist" to "least capitalist." Data limitations prevent doing this with every single nation. Nevertheless, it is possible to do it for about 140 of them, putting 35 nations into each of the four groups. Thus, among the top thirty-five "most capitalist" nations, in addition to the countries we mentioned earlier, many (but not all!) of the original members of the **European Union (EU)** would be included, along with Chile, Costa Rica, and Japan. At the other end of the spectrum, the economies of Ukraine, Algeria, Venezuela, and Zimbabwe would all fall into the group of the thirty-five "least capitalist" nations.

As we suggested earlier, people who live in the most capitalist nations in the world also tend to have the highest average income. For example, average per capita income for people living in the group including the thirty-five most capitalist nations averages over $31,000 per year. For people living in the next most capitalist group of nations, per capita income averages about $14,000 per year. Once we get down to the thirty-five least capitalist nations, average income has dropped to but $3,900 per year. And because rates of economic growth are *also* higher in more capitalist nations, the differences in income between the most and least capitalist nations are growing over time.[1]

Of course, this is a chapter about poverty, and the *average* income in a nation may bear little relation to the income earned by its poorest residents. Many people believe, for example, that capitalist nations promote excessively competitive behavior so that people who are not good at competing end up much poorer in capitalist than in noncapitalist nations. If the rich get richer in capitalist countries while the poor get poorer, then even if the average person in capitalist nations is doing well, the same might not be true for people at the bottom of the income distribution. As it turns out, however, the poor do *not* do worse in capitalist countries; in fact, they do *better*.

CAPITALISM AND POVERTY

Consider the thirty-five most capitalist nations in the world. On average, the poorest 10 percent of the population receives about 2.5 percent of total income in these countries. Indeed, if we look across *all* countries, we see that although there is some variation from nation to nation,

---

1 All income comparisons are made using a method called **purchasing power parity (PPP)**, generally acknowledged to be the most accurate means of making comparisons across nations with very different income levels and consumption bundles.

the poorest 10 percent of the population typically gets between 2.0 and 2.5 percent of total income. One way to put this is that on average, capitalism does *not* lower the share of total income going to the people at the bottom of the income distribution. Capitalist or Communist, in Africa or in the Americas, the per capita income of the poorest 10 percent of the population in a nation ends up being about one-quarter of per capita income in the middle of the income distribution for that country.

Now if you followed the numbers earlier about average income and capitalism, you may already have figured out the next point: Because capitalism raises total income in a nation without reducing the *share* of income going to the poor, capitalism ends up raising income at *all* points in the income distribution. Thus, for the poorest 10 percent of the population in highly capitalist countries, average per capita income is about $8,700 per year (or just under $35,000 per year for a family of four). For the poorest 10 percent of the population in the least capitalist countries, average income is under $950 per year (about $3,800 for a family of four). Expressed somewhat differently, poor people in the most capitalist nations can expect average income levels *eight times higher* than poor people in the least capitalist nations.

The radically better standard of living experienced by the poor in capitalist nations is reflected in many other statistics indicative of quality of life. For example, life expectancy in the thirty-five most capitalist nations is about 79 years; in the least capitalist, it is about 58. Similarly, infant mortality rates are *eight times higher* in the least capitalist countries than in the most capitalist countries. Moreover, because people at the top of the income distribution have access to health care in both rich and poor nations, these differences in life expectancy and infant mortality are chiefly due to differences among people at the bottom of the income distribution. In capitalist nations, compared to noncapitalist countries, it is the poor whose newborns are surviving infancy and whose adults are surviving to old age.

There is another compelling difference between capitalist and noncapitalist countries that sheds light on what the future may bring. In the thirty-five most capitalist countries of the world, fewer than 1 percent of children under the age of 15 are working rather than in school. In the thirty-five least capitalist nations, one child of every six under the age of 15 is working rather than being in school—a rate nearly twenty times higher. Thus, in capitalist nations, children are much more likely to be getting the education necessary for them to learn the skills of the future. This in turn means that **economic growth** is likely to be higher in capitalist nations than in noncapitalist nations, and this is exactly what we observe. Growth in per capita income in the thirty-five most capitalist countries averages about 2.3 percent per year, enough to double income at all levels over the next 30 years. In contrast, average per capita incomes are actually *falling* in the least capitalist countries, implying that the misery of today's poor in these nations is likely to get worse.

MORE THAN NUMBERS

It is easy to get too wrapped up in numbers, so it may be useful to make a few simple head-to-head comparisons. Consider North Korea and South Korea. Both emerged from World War II with shattered economies, only to fight each other in the Korean War. When the war was over, South Korea embraced capitalism, building an economy based on the rule of law, secure property rights, and a reliance on the market as the primary means of allocating scarce resources. North Korea rejected all of these, choosing instead a Communist system that relied on centralized command and control to allocate resources—a system ruled not by law but by one man at the top. South Korea became a world economic powerhouse, with per capita income of almost $28,000 per year. North Korea stagnated and, with a per capita income of only $1,800 per year, must now rely on foreign aid to feed many of its people.

If we were to look at East Germany and West Germany between World War II and the fall of the Berlin Wall in 1989, we would see the same story repeated. West Germany embraced the central principles of a market-based capitalist economy and prospered. East Germany rejected those principles, and its people were impoverished. A similar tale of two countries can be told in comparing the economies of Taiwan and China between 1950 and 1980: Capitalist Taiwan prospered while Communist China stagnated—and people at the bottom of the income distribution suffered the most.

Indeed, China itself presents us with a tale of two countries: the Communist version before 1980 and the increasingly capitalist one of the years since. After decades of post–World War II stagnation under communism, the gradual move toward market-based resource allocation in China since 1980 is transforming life for people at all levels of income. Overall, real per capita income has roughly doubled every decade since 1980. Moreover, at least in those areas of the country where the Communists have let the capitalists try their hand, this economic progress has been widespread and sustained. So even though political freedom in China is not yet to be had, the growing economic freedom in that nation is having the same impact it has had around the world and over time: When people are able to enjoy secure property rights, the rule of law, and a reliance on markets as allocators of scarce resources, people at *all* points in the distribution benefit.

FOR CRITICAL ANALYSIS

1. The income measures discussed in this chapter do not include noncash benefits that are often available to low-income individuals, such as food stamps and Medicaid. Do you think such noncash benefits are more likely to be made available to poor people in a rich nation or in a poor nation? Explain your answer. *Hint:* Do people get more or less charitable as their incomes rise? Then ask yourself, how will the difference in noncash benefits in rich nations versus poor nations affect your conclusions regarding relative incomes of poor individuals in capitalist nations compared to noncapitalist nations? Explain this answer as well.

2. How would a political system in which there is the rule of law (i.e., in which the same rules apply to everyone) serve to protect people at the bottom of the income distribution most strongly?

3. In light of the analysis in Chapter 1 and the information presented in this chapter, what are some ways that people in developed nations might help people in developing nations achieve higher income levels? Explain, giving specific examples, if you can.

4. If capitalism is so good at creating economic prosperity, why don't more nations try it?

5. Over the past few years, the United States has slipped downward in the rankings of capitalist countries. As you read the rest of this book, compile a list of the reasons you think the U.S. ranking has dropped.

6. According to the *CIA Factbook,* the Democratic Republic of the Congo is the poorest nation in the world. How do you suppose this country ranks in terms of its degree of capitalism? Test your prediction by going to the Fraser Institute's Web site (www.fraserinstitute.org) and seeing where the Congo rates on the Institute's Index of Economic Freedom.

CHAPTER 5

The Threat to Growth

Government spending has hit levels virtually unprecedented in American history. The federal government, for example, has been spending fully *one-quarter* of gross domestic product (GDP). But state and local governments have been spending nearly as much. Local government spending, for example, has accounted for 10 percent of GDP, while state governments have been spending about 12.5 percent. At no time in American history have state and local governments spent as much as they have been recently. Only briefly, during the height of World War II, has federal spending as a share of GDP ever rivaled its recent heights. Bailouts, TARPs, subsidies, entitlements, bloated pensions, subsidized health care, and two ground wars in Asia (Iraq and Afghanistan) have created a "perfect storm" of massive government spending at all levels.

THE BIG PICTURE

"So what," you might say. If the government wasn't spending it, someone else would be. Indeed, when government spends more, whatever the spending is on, there is ultimately only one place the government can obtain the resources. That place is you and everyone else who earns income each year in the United States. In the short run, just as you can borrow, so too can governments, an activity that is called running a **budget deficit.** Nevertheless, the ability to borrow does not change the fundamental **budget constraint** facing our society. What is spent today must be paid for now or in the future. And when it is government doing the spending, that means that higher spending today *must* eventually be matched with higher taxes. Hence, today's big spending means higher taxes (and lower private spending) for you and everyone else who earns income in the United States.

Now, if those higher taxes just meant that Peter would have less spending power so that Paul could have more, this chapter probably wouldn't be worth writing. But Peter's income does not simply appear like a surprise birthday gift. Instead, his income is the result of hard work, investing, and innovation. And when taxes rise, the **incentives** of taxpayers to engage in these activities is reduced—and that in turn means lower economic growth and lower wealth now and in the future.

INCENTIVES ARE IMPORTANT

We have seen in the previous chapters that secure property rights and the rule of law are crucial in fostering economic growth. These institutions help ensure that individuals are secure in the knowledge that they will get to keep the fruits of their labor. Hence, people are willing to work hard, invest for the future, and engage in innovation. And because all of these activities contribute to higher incomes and greater economic growth, they ensure more long-run prosperity. But note the key point. People undertake work, invest, and innovate because they believe they will be rewarded with the fruits of their efforts. If these fruits are denied them—because, for example, taxes take much of what they produce—the incentives to work, invest, and innovate are sharply reduced, and so too is economic growth and, ultimately, wealth.

Data from Europe illustrate how taxes shape incentives to work. Researchers have found that a tax increase of just over 12 percentage points induces the average adult in Europe to reduce work effort by over 120 hours per year—the equivalent of almost four weeks' work. Such a tax change also causes a sharp reduction in the number of people who work at all, and causes many others to join the **underground economy** (see Chapter 2), or to devote their time to **tax evasion.** Overall, then, higher tax rates cause lower output and higher unemployment. Wealth is reduced now and in the future.

Taxes also affect the incentives to invest. A good case in point is Ireland, whose economy in the 1980s was a disaster, and whose citizens were among the poorest of **European Union (EU)** citizens. In the 1990s, the Irish slashed the corporate **profits** tax to 12.5 percent, the lowest in Europe and only about one-third as high as the U.S. rate of 35 percent. Beginning in 2004, the Irish government also began offering a 20 percent tax credit for company spending on research and development, offering high-tech firms an opportunity to cut their taxes by starting up and expanding operations in Ireland. Almost immediately, Ireland became a magnet for new investment and for successful companies that didn't want to hand over one-third or more of their profits to the tax collector.

The combination of lower corporate tax rates and tax breaks on research and development induced hundreds of multinational corporations to begin operations in Ireland. They brought with them hundreds of thousands of new jobs (and this to a nation of only 4 million residents), and Ireland quickly became number one among the **EU's** fifteen original members in being home to companies that conduct research and development. And as for the people of Ireland, their per capita incomes went from the bottom ranks of the EU to the top.[1]

INNOVATION IS ESSENTIAL

On one point, all economists agree. Innovation is a fundamental, indeed necessary, element of economic growth. And note that we say "innovation" rather than "invention." The latter is the creation of a new idea—but plenty of new ideas go nowhere. Innovation is the transformation of a new idea into successful commercial, scientific, or artistic application. Although innovation may incorporate invention, it need not do so. A simple example may suffice.

Many people credit Thomas Edison with the invention in 1880 of the incandescent light bulb. In fact, the first recognizable incandescent bulb was created in 1802 by Sir Humphry Davy and a bulb very much like Edison's was patented in 1875 by two Canadians. Shortly after Edison independently patented an incandescent bulb, he bought the Canadians' patent rights from them for $5,000 (over $1 million in today's dollars)—and then proceeded to implement indoor electric lighting across America and around the world. The invention was the incandescent light bulb. The innovation entailed the successful commercial application of that invention, an activity that included power generation and transmission, as well as the widespread commercial distribution of the bulbs themselves. Sitting in an English, Canadian, or New Jersey laboratory, the bulb was a bright idea. But once it lit up millions of homes and workplaces, it raised the world's wealth and contributed to sustained economic growth that continues to enrich us today.

INNOVATION AND WEALTH

Steve Jobs (Apple) didn't invent the semiconductor, Bill Gates (Microsoft) didn't invent the computer operating system, Oprah Winfrey (The Oprah Show) didn't invent the talk show, and Mark

---

1 Sadly for the Irish, their government has decided to spend much of this higher income propping up mismanaged Irish banks who overinvested in commercial and residential real estate prior to the latest recession.

Zuckerman (Facebook) did not invent social networking. Yet each of these people became multi-billionaires as innovators in their respective fields of work. To be sure, each have come up with plenty of new ideas, but what distinguishes them from all of the inventors you have never heard of is that all of the people on the list above have developed and applied their ideas and others' in ways that created enormous commercial success. In doing so, each got rich. But more importantly for our purposes, all of these people have contributed significantly to the wealth of millions of *other* people around the world, by creating products that satisfied human wants.

Indeed, if we look more carefully at the world, we find that innovation is the source of most of our wealth. Somewhere along the line, whether it was the Mexican farmers who 6,000 years ago began genetically engineering the precursors to corn, or Bill Hewlett and David Packard, who transformed semiconductors into calculators, business machines, and laser printers, it is innovation that has created the products that enable us to live like no other species on earth. And although it is unlikely that many of the long-dead creators of corn got rich, many of the richest people in the world are that rich because of their innovations.

Even among the merely prosperous people of the world, innovation often plays a key role in creating their prosperity. Although **wealth** is obviously passed down from one generation to another, when we look at the **standard of living** of individuals, very little of that standard of living is determined by the financial inheritance they received from their ancestors. Instead, current living standards of people are primarily determined by the incomes they have earned for themselves. These incomes are chiefly the result of what they have produced in the workplace.[2] And most often, very high levels of workplace productivity are the result of innovative activity by those productive individuals.

TAXATION AND INNOVATION

Surely many things motivate all individuals, including innovators, great and small. One of these motivating factosrs may reasonably be assumed to be financial success. (We say this because there is a vast body of evidence that financial success is one of the motivators of human beings in virtually all walks of life.) This notion brings us back to taxes, where

---

2 We do inherit plenty of nonfinancial wealth from our parents, of course, including intelligence and work habits, which play a role in determining how much we produce and hence our standard of living. The importance of productivity is most obvious when we look at professional sports, where pay is quite obviously importantly determined by easily measurable criteria of productivity (such as touchdowns, home runs, or rebounds).

our story began. Innovators, like everyone else, only receive **after-tax income,** that is, income *after* the various government entities have collected the taxes they impose. These taxes may come in a variety of forms: income taxes, sales taxes, property taxes, and so forth. But whatever their form or level of government at which they are levied, higher taxes mean lower after-tax incomes. And this in turn means reduced incentives. Perhaps most importantly, the change in incentives reduces the incentive to innovate. But higher taxes also reduce the incentive to invest (because taxes cut into the after-tax income from investment) and even to work—because higher taxes mean lower after-tax income from work.

An easy way to think about the effect of taxes on behavior is to imagine that we decided to raise taxes on professional athletes. Recall from above that the most productive people are those who tend to earn the highest incomes. Almost surely, then, the biggest burden of higher taxes would be on those with the highest incomes—which also means those who are the most productive. The best runners and rebounders and hitters and passers would get the biggest increase in tax bills. What are the likely consequences? Overall performance would suffer. Athletes would spend less time working out in the off-season. They would spend less time practicing year round. They would devote less effort to studying their opponents—the list goes on and on. And the result would be a decline in the quality of the competition and less enjoyment for fans. Output, no matter how we measure it, would fall. To be sure, many players would still be motivated by pride and inherent competitive drive, but the extra edge offered by financial rewards would be gone—and so would the performance edge.

The same destruction of incentives occurs when taxes are raised on anyone who works, or invests, or innovates. As long as incomes are determined chiefly by performance (and the evidence is that they are), higher taxes reduce the incentive of people to engage in those activities that contribute to economic growth and thus increase our wealth. As in sports, the outcome is reduced performance and lower output, however measured.

THE RELEVANCE FOR TODAY

We started this chapter by discussing the historically high levels of government spending that we have been experiencing. Because this spending must eventually be paid for out of taxes, we can now see the threat to economic growth and prosperity that is posed by high levels of government spending. The result of this spending *must* be higher taxes, and higher taxes will reduce the incentives to work, invest, and innovate.

And this means less economic growth and lower income and wealth. Our standard of living in the future will be lowered because of our governments' spending today. Nearly a half century ago, President John F. Kennedy said, "An economy hampered by restrictive taxes will never produce enough revenue to balance our budget, just as it will never produce enough jobs or enough profits." Sadly, this is a message that our current political leaders do not seem to understand.

FOR CRITICAL ANALYSIS

1. President Obama campaigned on the theme that he would reduce taxes for 95 percent of working Americans. Why would such a campaign promise be difficult to put into practice?

2. Many European countries have imposed a **wealth tax.** It is typically based on everything a person owns minus everything the person owes (the difference between what is owned and what is owed is called **net worth**). Put yourself in the shoes of an individual in a country that has just decided to impose a wealth tax. How does a wealth tax affect your incentive to accumulate wealth? How does it affect your incentive to work hard?

3. Explain why the incentives of individuals and businesses are chiefly affected by changes in **marginal tax rates**—that is, the percentage of the *next* income they earn that they must pay in taxes.

4. Fifty years ago in America, high-income people paid 91 cents in federal personal income taxes on each additional dollar of income they earned. If you found yourself paying such a 91 marginal tax rate, how great would be your incentive to find legal **loopholes** to reduce your federal tax **liabilities?** If you found yourself in the lowest federal personal income tax bracket of, say, 15 percent (paying 15 cents in taxes out of each additional dollar earned), would your incentive to find loopholes to reduce your tax bill be the same? Explain.

5. Let's suppose that income tax rates rise significantly over the next ten years. How can people at all levels of income react over time, not just immediately after taxes are raised? How will the size of the response differ, say, a year after the rise in tax rates compared to a week after the increase? Is it possible that some people will actually change their behavior *before* the higher tax rates go into effect? Explain.

6. How does the structure of a country's tax system affect who decides to immigrate into the nation or emigrate out of the nation? Contrast, for example, nations A and B. Assume that nation A applies a 20 percent tax rate on every dollar of income earned by an individual (i.e., 20 cents in taxes must be paid on each dollar of income). Nation B applies a 10 percent tax rate (10 cents per dollar) on the *first* $40,000 per year of income and a 40 percent tax rate (40 cents per dollar) on all income *above* $40,000 per year earned by an individual. Start by computing the tax bill in each country that must be paid by a person earning $40,000 per year and the tax bill that must be paid by a person earning $100,000 per year. Then consider the more general issue: If the language, culture, and climate of the two nations are similar, and if a person can choose to live on one side or the other of a river separating the two nations, who is more likely to choose to live in A, and who is more likely to choose to live in B? To what extent does your reasoning apply if an ocean, rather than a river, separates the two countries? Does it apply if the language, culture, or climate in the two nations differs? Explain.

PART TWO

The Business Cycle, Unemployment, and Inflation

CHAPTER 6

Is GDP What We Want?

Economists disagree about a lot. One important point of disagreement has to do with how to measure things. For example, suppose you were interested in how the economy was doing, either over time or in comparison to other nations. Or perhaps you want to know how well different people across the country feel they are doing. Perhaps the most common way of addressing such issues would be with a measure linked to **gross domestic product (GDP).** For example, almost all macroeconomic policy is driven by policymakers' perceptions of what is happening to a few key variables, and GDP is on just about everyone's list of key variables. Moreover, as you saw in Chapter 4, the human condition varies dramatically around the globe. Radical differences in prosperity and poverty from one nation to the next can be understood only if we begin with a clear awareness of what is being measured. And that measurement starts with GDP.

WHAT DOES GDP MEASURE?

GDP is defined as the market value of new, domestically produced, final goods and services. There are four key elements of this definition:

1. *Market value*—GDP is calculated by multiplying the prices of goods and services by their quantities. Thus, it can move up or down just because of changes in the prices of goods and service. Most of our discussion will focus on **real GDP,** which adjusts GDP for changes in the **price level.** This way, we know that we are talking about the actual amounts of goods and services that are being produced.

2. *New*—The only goods and services that get into GDP are ones that are newly produced during the current accounting period, which normally is the current calendar year. Even though used cars, old houses, and even antiques are a source of satisfaction for many people, GDP focuses on those goods and services that are currently produced.

3. *Domestically produced*—If you were to look carefully at the components of a new car, you would find that much of that car was actually made in other nations, even if it is an "American" car. Similarly, much of the typical "Japanese" car sold in America is actually made in America. The GDP of a nation includes only those parts of cars (and other goods and services) that are made in that nation.

4. *Final goods and services*—Lots of intermediate steps go into producing goods and services, and typically many of these steps show up as separate transactions across the country. But because the value of each intermediate step is embedded in the value of the final product, we include only that final value in our measure of GDP. Otherwise, we would be double counting the final good and all of the components that go into it.

IMPUTED AND MISSING INFORMATION

Real GDP, that is, GDP corrected for changes in the price level, is the official measure of the new, domestically produced, final goods and services in an economy. Although this number is widely used for many purposes, you should be aware of its limitations. First, some important parts of it are "imputed," or estimated, by the officials at the government agency that publishes the GDP numbers. For example, even though there is no "market" in owner-occupied housing, the Commerce Department has devised methods of estimating the implicit rental value of houses occupied by their owners, and it includes the aggregate value of these services in the published measure of real GDP. In a similar vein, farmers consume some of the food items they produce before those items ever get to the market. Again, the Commerce Department has devised ways to estimate the amount of such food. As with owner-occupied housing, these estimates are included in the official GDP numbers.

Despite the government's best efforts, there are some major omissions from published measures of real GDP. For example, do-it-yourself activities are not included in the official measures, even though they constitute the production of a service. If you take your car to a mechanic, the services performed on the car end up as part of measured real GDP.

But if you and a friend repair your car, these services are not included in the statistics. The biggest category of do-it-yourself services left out of the official GDP statistics consists of those performed in the house by homemakers. It is widely estimated, for example, that the *weekly* value of a homemaker's services is several hundred dollars, none of which is included in the official figures for real GDP.

Then there is the matter of the huge volume of transactions—hundreds of billions of dollars per year—in markets for illegal and underground activities. In some "true" measure of real GDP, we should probably add in these activities, which include prostitution and the illegal drug trade, because such goods and services presumably generate satisfaction to the individuals purchasing them. We should also include "underground" income that is the result of legal activities but is not reported. (See Chapter 2 for more on this.) Some of this income goes unreported by individuals hoping to evade income taxes. But it also includes much of the income earned by illegal immigrants, who do not report their incomes simply because they do not wish to be deported.

ARE SUBTRACTIONS NECESSARY, TOO?

If we were able to adjust for the items mentioned in the previous section, we might agree that we have a solid measure of real GDP. Nevertheless, we might also feel that we should make some adjustments to real GDP to get a more accurate notion of the level of our material standard of living. For example, the government statisticians treat as equivalent the $5 you spend on gasoline to go on a date in the evening and the $5 you spend on gasoline for your trip to work in the morning. Clearly, however, most people would not think about these two expenditures in the same way.

The next category of items we might focus on is sometimes referred to as "regrettable necessities." This includes diplomacy, national security, police and fire protection, and prison facilities. These items typically don't yield consumer satisfaction in and of themselves. They are produced because they make it possible for us to enjoy the consumption of other goods. In this sense, we can think about regrettable necessities as intermediate goods that go into the production of other goods. As such, they probably should be subtracted from real GDP to get to a better measure of the final goods relevant to individuals, but the government statisticians won't hear of it.

It is also important to recognize that our urbanized, industrialized society has some drawbacks. Big cities make large-scale commercial activities (and thus more market goods) feasible. But they also bring with them a variety of urban disamenities, such as congestion, noise, and litter. If we are interested in some measure of welfare, we should make deductions from real GDP for such sources of dissatisfaction. (The same reasoning applies to pollution in general.) It is difficult to put a precise numerical value on them, however, and so none of the official statistics are adjusted.

WHAT DOES GDP TELL US?

At this point you might well be wondering whether real GDP has any link at all to what we might think of as happiness or welfare. After all, if the time you spend tinkering on your classic car is *excluded* from real GDP, while the gas you burn stuck in traffic every morning is *included* in real GDP, it almost seems as though the government accountants have things upside down and backwards. Just as importantly, plenty of the items that are important on our GDP (fast food, for example) are a negligible part of GDP in other countries, while the items that are important to them (say, cassava root) are almost unknown to most of us. What, then, can we learn from comparisons of real GDP across nations? (The same query might be asked about comparisons of different time periods *within* a country. Whale oil was a big deal in 1840, just as laptop computers matter a lot today.)

For many years, economists thought that such comparisons, even though routinely made, might just as routinely mean nothing. Imagine, for example, that economies with lots more goods and services were also saddled with lots more crime and pollution and lots less leisure time. Under these circumstances, real GDP might bear no relationship whatsoever to the welfare, happiness, or satisfaction experienced by different people in different lands, or by people at different points in time in the same country. As it turns out, however, it now appears that real GDP might actually be quite useful in making these comparisons across people and countries, and over time.

BRINGING IN HAPPINESS

Even as economists have been busy measuring real GDP, a variety of other researchers—such as sociologists, psychologists, and political scientists—have been asking people how happy or satisfied they are with their lives. Now, answers to questions such as these always need to be taken with a grain of salt and a dose of caution because "talk is cheap." That is, when you go to the store to buy something, you must make a real sacrifice to obtain the item. But when a person conducting a poll asks you whether you are happy or unhappy, it costs no more to check the box next to "happy" than it does to check the box next to "unhappy."

Keeping this caution in mind, economists Betsey Stevenson and Judson Wolfers thought it might be useful to see if there was any link between measures of real GDP and measures of happiness. Obviously, some adjustments were in order even before beginning. For example, some countries are large and some are small, so the researchers divided real GDP by population in each nation to obtain **real GDP per capita**. Similarly, the exact questions asked of people differed across nations and over time, so considerable work was needed to put all of the answers on a comparable footing. After all of this was done, however, the results were striking.

REAL GDP AND HAPPINESS ARE STRONGLY LINKED

Stevenson and Wolfers found that there is a strong and consistent positive relationship between real GDP per capita and reported levels of happiness. Using data spanning many decades, and covering well over one hundred countries, the authors show that when per capita real GDP is higher, reported measures of satisfaction or happiness are higher also. Notably, there is no "satiation" point—that is, it appears that even the richest and happiest peoples have the opportunity to become even happier as their incomes rise further.

The authors examine the data in three different ways. First, they look at measures of income (real GDP per capita) and happiness (or reported well-being) across different people within the same country at one point in time. Then they examine income and well-being across different countries at the same point in time. And finally, they assess real per capita GDP and happiness over long periods of time within given countries. In each case, they observe the same strong positive relationship: People with higher real per capita incomes report being happier.

Obviously, real income is not the only factor that influences happiness. Gender, age, and many difficult-to-measure variables are important also. Moreover, it is entirely possible that some other factor is responsible for simultaneously creating high levels of income and happiness. For example, in Chapter 4 we noted that secure property rights and the rule of law are important in creating high levels of real GDP per capita. It may be the case that these same institutions also happen to make people happier, perhaps because they enhance personal liberty. Nevertheless, even though it may be true that "money can't buy happiness," the results of Stevenson and Wolfers make one point clear: Despite all of its imperfections, real GDP per capita is strongly linked to well-being, at least as perceived by the human beings being asked about such matters. And so, although GDP may not be a perfect measure of anything, we keep on using it because it seems to beat all of the alternatives.

FOR CRITICAL ANALYSIS

1. How does one determine what is a final good or service and what is a regrettable necessity or an intermediate good? In other words, where does one draw the line?

2. Why is it important to carefully distinguish between GDP and real GDP?

3. Would you categorize each of the following expenditures as intermediate goods, regrettable necessities, or consumption goods: (a) a spare tire, (b) surgery to repair a badly broken arm, (c) a Botox injection to remove forehead wrinkles, (d) voice lessons, and (e) expenditures on your college education? Explain your reasoning in each case. Would your answers to (c) and (d) change if you knew that the purchaser was a professional singer who made many public appearances? Why or why not?

4. Over the past 40 years, growing numbers of women have entered the labor force, becoming employed outside the home. As a result, many women now hire people to do household tasks (such as child-care and house cleaning) that they used to do themselves. What impact does this "hiring out" of household tasks have on measures on GDP? Explain.

5. Over the past 40 years, the levels of water and air pollution in the United States have declined substantially in the United States. Would these environmental improvements likely be reflected in reported measures of well-being or happiness? Would they likely be reflected in GDP?

6. Are nations with large underground economies likely to be happier or unhappier than one would expect, given their *measured* levels of real per capita GDP? Explain.

CHAPTER 7

What's in a Word? Plenty, When It's the "R" Word

Incumbent presidents (and members of their political party) hate the "R" word. We speak here of **recession,** a word used to describe a downturn or stagnation in overall, nationwide economic activity. Politicians' attitudes toward recessions are driven by the simple fact that people tend to "vote their pocketbooks." That is, when the economy is doing well, voters are likely to return incumbent politicians to office, but when the economy is doing poorly, voters are likely to "throw the bums out." Interestingly, although *recession* is the word most commonly used to describe a period of poor performance by the economy, most people don't really know what the word means.

THE NBER

Ever since its founding in 1920, a private organization called the National Bureau of Economic Research (NBER) has sought to accurately measure the state of overall economic conditions in the United States. (It also sponsors research on other economic issues.) Over time, the NBER developed a reputation for measuring the economy's performance in an evenhanded and useful way. As a result, most people now accept without argument what the NBER has to say about the state of the economy. And most notably, this means that it is the NBER that we rely on to tell us when we are in a recession.

If you are an avid reader of newspapers, you may have heard a recession defined as any period in which there are at least two quarters (three-month periods) of declining **real gross domestic product (real GDP).** In fact, the NBER's recession-dating committee places little reliance on the performance of real (inflation-adjusted) GDP when deciding on the state of the economy. There are two reasons for this. First, the government measures GDP only on a quarterly basis, and the NBER prefers to focus on more timely data that are available at least monthly. Second, the official GDP numbers are subject to frequent and often substantial revisions, so what once looked like good economic performance might suddenly look bad, and vice versa.

Looking back at 2001 (a turbulent year), for example, the initial figures showed that real GDP declined in only one quarter during the year. But when the government finally finished all of its revisions to the data, it turned out that real GDP actually fell during *three* quarters of 2001. In 2007, the government issued a revision of its revised GDP figures for 2004–2006. Of the twelve quarters covered by this "revision of the revisions," the numbers for all twelve were changed: Two were revised upward and ten downward. One can easily see why an organization such as the NBER, which prides itself on reliability and accuracy, might be reluctant to place too much weight on measures of real GDP.

So what does the NBER use as its criteria in measuring a recession? Its official definition of a recession gives us some insight: "A recession is a significant decline in activity spread across the economy, lasting more than a few months, visible in industrial production, employment, real income, and wholesale–retail sales." Those are a lot of words to define just one term, but it's not too difficult to get a handle on it. The point to note at the outset is that the NBER focuses chiefly on four separate pieces of information:

- Industrial production
- Employment
- Real income (measured by inflation-adjusted personal income of consumers)
- Sales at both the wholesale and retail levels

All of these figures are reliably available on a monthly basis, and so every month, the NBER uses the latest figures on each to take the pulse of the economy. When all four are moving upward, that's generally good news. When all are moving downward, that's definitely bad news. And when some are moving in one direction and some in another direction, that's when expert judgment comes into play.

THE THREE *D*'S

If the NBER recession-dating committee uses a strict formula to time the onset or end of a recession, the committee members don't reveal what it is. What they do reveal is that they are looking for three crucial elements, all starting with the letter *D,* when they officially announce the start or end of a recession:

1. *Depth.* If there is a downturn in one or more of the four key variables, the NBER focuses first on the magnitude of that downturn. For example, in an economy like ours with total employment of over 140 million, a drop in employment of 50,000 would not be crucial. But an employment drop of, say, one million surely would be considered significant.

2. *Duration.* Month-to-month fluctuations in economic activity are the norm in our economy. These fluctuations occur partly because our measures of economic activity are imperfect and partly because, in an economy as complex as ours, many things are happening all the time that have the capacity to affect the overall performance of the economy. Thus, if real personal income moves up or down for a month or even two months in a row, the recession-dating committee is likely to determine that such a change is well within the bounds of normal variation. But if a trend persists for, say, six months, the committee is likely to place a much heavier weight on that movement.

3. *Dispersion.* Because the NBER is trying to measure the overall state of the economy, it wants to make sure it is not being misled by economic developments that may be important to many people but are not reliable indicators of the overall state of the economy. For example, America is becoming less dependent on industrial production and more reliant on service industries. In addition, it is well known that industrial production is sensitive to sharp movements not shared by sectors elsewhere in the economy. So the NBER tempers the importance of industrial production by simultaneously relying on measures such as wholesale and retail sales to make sure it has a picture of what is happening throughout the economy.

A Precise Answer

Having blended its four measures of the economy in a way that reflects its focus on the three *D*'s, the recession-dating committee makes its decision. A recession, in its view, begins "just after the economy reaches a peak of activity" and ends "as the economy reaches its trough" and starts expanding again. Between trough and peak, the economy is said to be in an **expansion.** Historically, the normal state of the economy is expansion. Most recessions are brief (usually ending within 12–18 months), and in recent decades, they have been rare. Our most recent recession began in December 2007 after six years of economic expansion, and ended in June 2009.

The four measures used by the NBER to date recessions generally move fairly closely together. Although individually they sometimes give conflicting signals for short periods of time, they soon enough start playing the same song. Nevertheless, some contention about the NBER's decisions remains. There are two sources of debate. One focuses on *potential* growth of economic activity, and the other highlights the importance of population growth.

The NBER defines a recession as an absolute decline in economic activity. But some economists note that at least for the past couple of centuries, growth in economic activity from year to year has been the norm in most developed nations, including the United States. Hence, they argue, a recession should be declared whenever growth falls significantly below its long-term potential. This dispute becomes more important when there is reason to believe that potential growth has shifted for some reason or when comparing the current performance of two nations that are growing at different rates. For example, suppose nation X has potential growth of 4 percent per year while nation Y has potential growth of only 2 percent per year. If both are actually growing at 2 percent, the unemployment rate in X will be rising, and some people would argue that this fact is sufficient to declare that X is in a state of recession. The biggest problem with this proposed measure of recession is that it is difficult to declare with confidence exactly what the potential growth rate of any country is.

The second point of contention starts with the observation that the population is growing in most countries. Hence, even if economic activity is growing, the well-being of the average citizen might not be. For example, suppose the population is growing three percent per year but real personal income is growing only two percent per year. Assuming that the other measures of activity were performing like personal income, the NBER would say the economy was in an expansion phase, even though **real per capita income** was declining. Some economists would argue that this state of affairs should be declared a recession, given that the term is supposed to indicate a less-than-healthy economy. This point has some validity. Nevertheless, there have not been many prolonged periods when the NBER has said the economy was expanding while real per capita income was falling.

Ultimately, of course, even if the recession-dating committee somehow tinkered with its methods to better acknowledge the importance of potential growth and population changes, some other issue would undoubtedly be raised to dispute the NBER's conclusions. For now, most economists are content to rely on the NBER to make the call. Most politicians are, too—except, of course, when it suits them otherwise. As for ordinary voters, well, even if they don't know how a recession is defined, they surely know what one feels like—and are likely to vote accordingly.

For Critical Analysis

1. Why is it important, both for the political process and for our understanding of the economy, for the NBER to resist the temptation to change its definition of a recession to fit the latest political pressures or economic fads?

2. Do you think that voters care more about whether the NBER says the economy is in a state of recession or whether they and their friends and family members are currently employed in good jobs? Why do politicians make a big deal over whether the economy is "officially" in a recession or an expansion? (*Hint:* Is it hard for the average voter to tell what is going on in the economy outside his or her community, leaving the voter dependent on simple measures— or labels—of what is happening elsewhere in the economy?)

3. Examine the data from the last six recessions. (Good sources for data are www.nber.org/cycles/recessions.html, www.bea.gov, and www.globalindicators.org.) Rank them on the basis of both duration and severity. The first is easy; the second is more difficult: Is it possible that some people—either politicians or other citizens—might disagree about how to measure the severity of a particular recession? How would you measure it?

4. Return to the data you examined for question 3. Some people have called the recession of 2007–2009 the "Great Recession." Based on the data you think most relevant, is this latest recession worthy of being singled out as "Great"? Explain.

5. The stock market has been called a "leading indicator" of future economic activity, while the unemployment rate has been called a "lagging indicator" of past economic activity. Combine the data from questions 3 and 4, including data on the stock market and the unemployment rate to answer the following two questions:

   (a) How well do movements in a stock price index (such as the DJIA or the S&P 500) predict ahead of time the beginning or end of each recession?

   (b) How well do beginnings or endings of recessions predict future changes, up or down, in the unemployment rate?

6. Why do we bother to declare the beginning or end of something called a "recession"?

CHAPTER **8**

The Great Recession

The period from 2004 to 2010 was arguably the most tumultuous in American history since the 1930s. We'll skip the details, but the year-by-year highlights shown in Table 8–1 should give you a flavor of the events that transpired over this recent period.

Home foreclosures hit record levels, millions of people lost their jobs, total output of goods and services fell by 6 percent, and the unemployment rate reached its highest level in nearly 30 years. Some people have even referred to the downturn of 2007–2009 as the "Great Recession." Was it really so bad, and if so, why? Just as importantly, what lessons can we learn for the future?

Table 8–1 Key Economic Events of the Years 2004–2010

Year	Events
2004	The Federal Reserve begins tightening monetary policy late in the year
2005	The buoyant housing market shows early signs of weakness
2006	Housing prices begin falling and foreclosures head upward
2007	Home foreclosures soar and the recession of 2007–2009 begins in December
2008	Widespread financial panic strikes in October and the recession deepens
2009	The recession ends in June after unemployment peaks at 10.1 percent
2010	Foreclosures continue but improving job market signals recovery is underway

48

The Years Before

The foundations for the recession of 2007–2009 were laid in policy choices by Congress over a long period leading up to the recession. In fact, we need to go back to 1995, when both Congress and the Clinton administration began pushing hard for banks and other mortgage-lending institutions to relax the standards applied to anyone seeking a home **mortgage.** The goal was to increase home ownership, particularly among lower-income U.S. residents.

Mortgage-lending institutions got the message. They began relaxing standards for down payments, credit histories, and other barometers of financial risk. Many of the new home loans they made were labeled subprime or Alt-A (so-called borderline mortgages). After the recession of 2001–2002, the two giant government-sponsored mortgage corporations, **Fannie Mae** and **Freddie Mac,** began pushing lenders to offer even more mortgage loans of dubious quality (see Chapter 15). Soon almost anyone could get a mortgage, and within a short period of time, a housing boom took flight. Low-income and even no-income individuals were realizing the American dream of home ownership—with lots of debt to pay back.

No lending institution, even the most risk-loving, would continue to make a larger and larger share of its loans to risky borrowers if it could not shift some or all of the risk elsewhere. Thus, financial firms invented and expanded a variety of securities to spread this risk. Included among these were:

- Mortgage-backed security (MBS)
- Asset-backed security (ABS)
- Collateralized debt obligation (CDO)

Although the details differed among them, all of these securities had the same organizing principle: A financial firm borrowed money using high-risk mortgages and other debts as collateral, and then lent the funds out to create more high-risk debts. The money kept flowing and the risks—which were considerable—were spread out over the many purchasers of these securities.

Downturn And Panic

Late in 2004 the Federal Reserve began tightening credit, and by 2005, interest rates had started up. Under ordinary circumstances, the change in Fed policy likely would have produced, at worst, a mild recession, such as we observed in 2000–2001. But conditions were not ordinary. Many of the mortgage loans made in 2003–2005 entailed relatively low initial monthly payments that sharply escalated after two to three years. When these payments began rising on a wide scale in late 2005 and early 2006, many borrowers could not make those higher payments, and the housing **bubble** burst with a vengeance. Individuals who had purchased homes hoping to sell them for a quick **profit** found themselves "underwater," that is, the market values of their properties were suddenly less than what they owed. Many borrowers just *abandoned* their houses, refusing to make any more payments on their mortgages.

All of the entities (individuals, firms, even governments) that owned MBSs, ABSs, and CDOs were suddenly receiving billions of dollars less in monthly mortgage payments. Moreover, it was clear that the market value of these securities and obligations was going to turn out to be less than people had anticipated. Within a few months, hundreds of billions of dollars' worth of perceived wealth simply vanished—gone, just like the millions of homeowners who simply walked away from their mortgages and their homes. By late 2007 consumer and business spending was down and the recession had begun. And in 2008 when people began to realize just how worthless many of the fancy MBSs, ABSs, and CDOs were going to be, a financial panic developed and soon spread around much of the world.

IN STEPS THE FED

Late in 2008, rapidly eroding confidence in America's financial system led to the near or total collapse of several major financial firms. Many commercial banks, investment banks, and even insurance companies were suddenly in dire condition, and potential borrowers across the country found themselves unable to obtain funds from anyone, at any rate of interest. The entire network of American financial markets was on the verge of a collapse that, if it had happened, might have produced conditions much like those experienced in the Great Depression of 1929–1933.

Mindful of the costs of inaction, the Fed moved swiftly to maintain and restore confidence in key components of the financial system. But its actions were considerably broader than ever before. Historically, for example, the Fed has lent funds to commercial banks and to the federal government itself. But in 2008, the Fed also lent hundreds of billions of dollars directly to nonbank corporations around the country. Moreover, the Fed began purchasing obligations of the government-sponsored mortgage market giants Fannie Mae and Freddie Mac, hoping to encourage more lending for home purchases. And finally, the Fed agreed to the following trade with commercial banks: It would exchange billions of dollars of risk-free federal **bonds** it held for billions of dollars of high-risk private bonds that they held. In effect, the Fed helped the banks remove high-risk assets of questionable value from their **balance sheets,** thus reducing the chances that skittish depositors might suddenly make large-scale withdrawals of funds from commercial banks.

The Fed's dramatic actions eventually brought the panic to a halt. Just as was envisioned when the Fed was created back in 1913, it served as a "lender of last resort" (see Chapter 20). The key difference compared to the past was that the Fed decided that practically *any* major company might qualify as worthy of lending by the Fed. While the long-run implications of this unprecedented change in Fed policy remain uncertain, one point is clear. The Fed's massive lending operations (which totaled over $1.5 *trillion*) halted the panic and prevented the recession from getting much worse.

How Bad Was It?

Even so, the recession of 2007–2009 was arguably worse than any other recession we've had since World War II. It also likely ranks among the half dozen or so worst we've had in our history. For example, during the latest recession, total employment fell 6 percent, compared to a mere 2 percent in the 2000–2001 recession, and 5 percent in 1948–1949, which had previously been the largest postwar drop. Similarly, total output in the economy fell 4.1 percent in 2007–2009. The largest prior decline in a postwar recession had been the 3.2 percent fall in 1973–1974. And although the unemployment rate (10.1 percent) did not get as high as it had in the 1981–1982 recession (10.8 percent), the jump in the unemployment rate was similar in both recessions—just over five percentage points.

By these measures, while the recession of 2007–2009 was large compared to other postwar recessions, it was minor compared to the Great Depression (1929–1933) and modest compared to the recessions of 1937–1938 and 1919–1920. But the latest recession will likely stick with the American people for a long time, for two well-deserved reasons. First, there is the matter of "what might have been" had the Federal Reserve not stepped in aggressively to end the financial panic of 2008. Many economists agree that if the Fed had not acted, the consequences could have rivaled those experienced in 1929–1933, when output fell 30 percent and the unemployment rate hit 25 percent.

Second, the housing market was utterly devastated in the recession of 2007–2009, to a degree not seen since the 1930s. Housing prices fell

40 percent, and millions of families lost their homes. The number of housing starts, which had previously peaked at two million per year, dropped to under 500,000. In many communities, housing constructions ground to a complete halt, often with houses simply left behind, partially finished.

MORE ON THE FED

Amid the chaos surrounding the financial panic and the recession, not many commentators paid much attention to two changes in Fed policy that enlarged on a massive scale its role in allocating resources. First, the Fed asked for and received from Congress the legal authority to pay interest on the **reserves** held by the banking system. For many years before, economists had argued that the Fed should have the authority to pay interest on banks' **required reserves** —that is, those reserves that banks are legally mandated to hold. But with the blessing of Congress, the Fed has gone further than this, by paying interest on **excess reserves** also—that is, on the reserves banks hold over and above the legally required minimum. The problem with paying interest on excess reserves is that it discourages banks from making loans to individuals and businesses. Faced with a choice of making risky loans to the private sector or collecting guaranteed, risk-free interest from the Fed, many banks chose the risk-free option. The result is that excess reserves soared from their level of a few billion dollars to amounts well in excess of a *trillion* dollars— funds that were not available to private sector borrowers. Thus, for long after the panic of 2008 was over, recovery from the recession was impeded because banks have been earning interest on their excess reserves rather than making productive but risky loans to the private sector.

The sluggish credit market led the Fed to announce that—for the first time in its history—it needed to get involved in making loans to entities other than commercial banks or the federal government. Thus, since the fall of 2008, the Federal Reserve has been allocating credit all over the country, deciding who shall get loans (and thus survive) and who shall not (and thus face economic ruin). Although the U.S. Treasury has been widely criticized for bailing out investment banks and automobile companies, the Fed has quietly been reshaping credit markets on a grand scale, while attracting almost no attention from the press. On a scale unprecedented in American history, hundreds of billions of dollars' worth of resources are being allocated behind the closed doors of the Federal Reserve System's headquarters in Washington, DC—for reasons known only to the politically appointed government officials doing the allocating.

WHAT HAVE WE LEARNED?

As we discuss more fully in Chapter 20, the latest recession confirms the pivotal role that the Federal Reserve can play when there is a financial panic. By acting as a lender of last resort, the Fed has the capacity to stave off economy-wide financial meltdowns. This was the role originally intended for the Fed back in 1913, and one that it failed to perform in 1929–1933. It is now clear that the Fed has the tools to do this should the need arise in the future.

A second key lesson of the recession of 2007–2009 is one that politicians don't seem to have absorbed. The attempts of Congress to artificially pump up home ownership in the United States chiefly encouraged financially ill-equipped individuals to purchase houses that they could not afford. When the housing market turned down, many of these people walked away from their obligations, with devastating consequences for the rest of the economy. Thus, Congressionally mandated housing policy set the stage for an unduly severe recession. There is no sign as yet, however, that the members of Congress recognize their role in this. The laws that encouraged high-risk lending to homeowners are still in place, and Fannie Mae and Freddie Mac are still doing their best to subsidize home purchases by individuals who are financially unprepared to meet their obligations. The risks of this policy are compounded by the Fed's decision to allocate credit on a grand scale throughout the economy. In America and elsewhere, government officials have a lousy historical track record when it comes to picking winners and losers in the marketplace. There is absolutely no reason that the officials at the Fed are likely to do any better—which means that many billions of dollars' worth of resources will likely end up being squandered by the Fed.

A third lesson is one that will only be learned in the future, likely sometime after you read these words. As we noted, the Fed engaged in roughly $1.5 trillion in new lending between late 2008 and 2010. In the long run, this is far more lending than the economy can possibly absorb without touching off a substantial inflation—perhaps one involving a *doubling* of the price level. No one thinks the Fed's intent is to permit such a massive increase in the price level, but no one is quite sure how the Fed will *avoid* it, without plunging the United States back into severe recession. Stay tuned, because by the end of the course in which you are using this book, economists will have a much better idea of how this next economic drama is going to work itself out.

FOR CRITICAL ANALYSIS

1. What elements of the recession of 2007–2009 have led many observers to refer to it as the Great Recession? Do you think this title is warranted? Explain, using data to back up your conclusions.

2. What members of Congress have the most to gain by passing laws that subsidize the purchase of homes by high-risk, low-income individuals? What data would you need to test your hypothesis?

3. During the recession, Congress changed the law on unemployment benefits to enable people to collect such benefits for up to 99 weeks (the limit had previously been 26 weeks). What impact do you think this change in the law had on (i) employment, (ii) the duration of unemployment, and (iii) the unemployment rate? Explain.

4. How will financial institutions and other borrowers pay off the loans made to them by the Fed during the recession? What consequences do you think this will have for the economy?

5. Other possible measures of the severity of a recession are (i) decline in manufacturing output, (ii) decline in retail sales, and (iii) duration of unemployment. Based on these criteria, how did the recession of 2007–2009 stack up to other post–World War II recessions?

6. In general, should policy makers be more concerned with high inflation or high unemployment? As you saw in Chapter 1, the inflation rate in Zimbabwe recently got up to 230 *million* percent per year, at the same time that the unemployment rate hit 80 percent of the workforce. Is it possible that the policy choices that yield a high inflation rate also eventually produce a high unemployment rate?

CHAPTER **9**

The Case of the Disappearing Workers

Every month, the Bureau of Labor Statistics (BLS) goes out into the labor market to determine how many unemployed people there are in the United States. With the data it acquires, the BLS calculates the **unemployment rate.** This number is a key indication of how well the economy is doing. The unemployment rate is calculated in a seemingly straightforward way: It is the percentage of the total **labor force** that is (1) aged 16 and older but not institutionalized or in school, and (2) actively seeking employment but has not found it.

The reelection chances of incumbent presidents often hinge on the estimated rate of unemployment. Historically, when the unemployment rate is rising, the president's chances of reelection have been far worse than when the rate is stable or falling. As the old saying goes, "people vote their pocketbooks" (or in this case, their pay stubs).

For this and a variety of other reasons, understanding how the unemployment rate is measured is important for politicians and ordinary citizens alike. Remarkably, however, there is little consensus about the accuracy of unemployment statistics in the United States. First, consider the period when the United States had its highest measured rate of unemployment—the Great Depression, which started in 1929 and did not fully end until a decade later.

TWENTY-FIVE PERCENT UNEMPLOYMENT—HARD TO IMAGINE

If you look at official government statistics on the unemployment rate during the Great Depression, you will find that in some statistical series, the rate hit 25 percent—meaning that one of every four Americans who were part of the labor force could not find a job during the depth of the depression. That high unemployment rate, of course, makes any **recession** since then seem insignificant in terms of the propostion of people adversely affected.

Some economists, though, are not so sure that one-fourth of the labor force was actually unemployed during the Great Depression. The reason is simple: At that time, the federal government had instituted numerous programs to "put people back to work." These included the Works Progress Administration (WPA), the Civilian Conservation Corps (CCC), and various lesser programs. Government statisticians decided that everyone working in these federally sponsored "make-work" programs would have been unemployed otherwise. Consequently, they decided to count these millions of Americans as unemployed. Michael Darby, an economist at UCLA, subsequently recalculated unemployment statistics for the depth of the Great Depression. After adjusting for people who were actually working but were counted as unemployed, he found a maximum unemployment rate of 17 percent. This number is still the highest we have had in modern times, but it is certainly not one-fourth of the labor force.

How much sense does Darby's adjustment make? The argument against the official government statistics is straightforward: The federal government taxed individuals and businesses to pay workers at the WPA and CCC. Had the federal government not levied the taxes to pay these new government employees, the private sector would have had more disposable income, more spending, and higher employment. Whether all of those people would have gotten private sector jobs is impossible to know, but it is clear that the official numbers greatly overstated the true unemployment rate during the Great Depression.

DISCOURAGED WORKERS: A COVER FOR A HIGHER "TRUE" UNEMPLOYMENT RATE?

Certain individuals, after spending some time in the pool of the unemployed, may become discouraged about their future job prospects. They may leave the labor market to go back to school, to retire, to work full-time at home without pay, or just to take some time off. Whichever path they choose, when interviewers from the BLS ask these individuals whether they are "actively looking for a job," they say no. Individuals such as these are often referred to as **discouraged workers.** They might seek work if labor market conditions were better and potential wages were higher, but they have decided that such is not the case, so they have left the labor market. For years, some critics of the officially measured unemployment rate have argued that during recessions, the rising numbers of discouraged workers cause the government to grossly underestimate the actual rate of unemployment.

To get a feel for the labor market numbers, let's look at the 1990s, perhaps one of the greatest periods of rising employment in U.S. history. During that decade, the number of Americans who were unemployed fell by over five million. Moreover, far fewer workers settled for part-time jobs. Many who had been retired came back to work, and many of those about to retire continued to work. There were even large numbers of students who left school to take high-paying jobs in the technology sector.

The onset of the 2001 recession produced a turnaround in all of those statistics. The number of unemployed rose by about 2.5 million individuals. The number of part-time workers who indicated that they would like to work full-time rose by over a million. And the proportion of those out of work for more than half a year increased by over 50 percent.

According to some economists, another two million workers dropped out of the labor force—the so-called discouraged-worker problem. For example, University of Chicago economist Robert Topel claims, "The unemployment rate does not mean what it did 20 years ago." He argues that employment opportunities for the least skilled workers no longer exist in today's labor market, so such individuals simply left the labor force, discouraged and forgotten by the statisticians who compile the official numbers.

ARE DISCOURAGED WORKERS A PROBLEM?

Other economists argue differently. They note that the labor market is no different from any other market, so we can examine it using **supply** and **demand** analysis, just as we do with any other good or service. The **labor supply curve** is upward-sloping. That means that as overall wages rise (corrected for inflation, of course), the quantity of labor supplied would be expected to increase. After all, when the inflation-corrected price of just about anything else goes up, we observe that the quantity supplied goes up, too. Therefore, argue these economists, the concept of discouraged workers is basically flawed. They say it makes no more sense to talk of discouraged workers than it would to talk of "discouraged apples" that are no longer offered for sale when the price of apples falls.

Because of the upward-sloping supply curve of labor, when **real wages** rise economy-wide, we expect that retirees and those about to retire will return to or remain in the labor market. We expect students to quit school early if the wages they can earn are relatively high. The opposite must occur when we go into a recession or the economy stagnates. That is, with reduced wage growth (or even declines in economy-wide real wages) and reduced employment opportunities, we expect more young people to stay in school longer, retirees to stay retired, and those about to retire to actually do so. In other words, we expect the same behavior in response to incentives that we observe in all other markets.

DISABILITY INSURANCE AND LABOR FORCE PARTICIPATION

It is also worth noting that some, perhaps many, of the departures from the labor force by low-skill individuals may actually be prompted by certain government programs. We refer here to a portion of the Social Security program that has expanded dramatically over the past 20 years. It involves **disability payments.** Originally established in 1956 as a program to help individuals under age 65 who are truly disabled, Social Security Disability Insurance (SSDI) has become the federal government's second fastest growing program (after Medicare). The real value of benefits has steadily risen as the Social Security Administration (SSA) gradually made it easier for individuals to meet the legal criteria for "disabled" status. SSDI now accounts for over $100 billion in federal spending per year. Under SSDI, even individuals who are not truly disabled can receive payments from the government when they do not work.

In addition, because Social Security also offers Supplemental Security Income (SSI) payments for disabled people who have little or no track record in the labor force, some people are calling disability insurance the centerpiece of a new U.S. welfare state. Since 1990, the number of people receiving disability payments from the SSA has more than tripled to over eight million—perhaps not surprising when you consider that the real value of the monthly benefits a person can collect has risen almost 60 percent in the past thirty-five years. The federal government now spends more on disability payments than on food stamps or unemployment benefits.

What does this mean? Simply that people who might have worked through chronic pain or temporary injuries—particularly those without extensive training and education—have chosen to receive a government disability benefit instead. The average Social Security disability payment is about $1,000 per month, tax-free. For many at the lower echelons of the job ladder, $1,000 per month tax-free seems pretty good. Indeed, those receiving disability payments make up the largest group of the two million or so who left the labor force during the 2001–2002 recession. We suspect that when analysts go back and look at the recession of 2007–2009, they'll find the same story. And because people respond to incentives, we can be sure of one thing: Whatever happens to the economy in the future, if the real value of disability payments keeps rising, so will the number of people with disabilities.

For Critical Analysis

1. To what extent do you believe that the existence of unemployment benefits increases the duration of unemployment and consequently the unemployment rate? (*Hint:* Use demand analysis and **opportunity cost.**)

2. Is it possible for the unemployment rate to be "too low"? In other words, can you conceive of a situation in which the economy would be worse off in the long run because there is not enough unemployment?

3. It is believed that much of the increase in the number of people collecting SSDI has resulted from decisions by workers at the Social Security Administration (SSA) to make it easier to qualify for benefits. How are the disability rules set by SSA workers likely to change depending on (a) whether the SSA budget is held constant or expands when the number of SSDI recipients rises, (b) the overall state of the economy, especially the unemployment rate, and (c) the likelihood that individuals with disabilities will be discriminated against in the workplace?

4. What would happen to the number of disabled people if Social Security disability payments were made subject to income taxes? Explain.

5. During the latest recession Congress increased the length of time people could receive unemployment benefits to 99 weeks (almost two years) from its previous level of 26 weeks (about six months). What impact do you think this change had on (i) the unemployment rate and (ii) the average duration of unemployment? Explain.

6. Imagine that at two different times—late 1933 (when the economy was struggling out of the depths of the Depression) and late 1939 (when the economy was expanding rapidly)—there were a million people on make-work government jobs who were officially classified as "unemployed." In which year (1933 or 1939) were these make-work employees more likely to have been displaced from private sector jobs and in which were they more likely to have been displaced from the ranks of the unemployed? Explain. How would this distinction factor into your thinking about whether such people should be officially classed as "employed" or "unemployed"? Explain.

CHAPTER 10

Poverty, Wealth, and Equality

In 1960, the poorest 20 percent of households in the United States received a bit over four percent of total income. Today, after half a century of government efforts to relieve poverty, the bottom 20 percent receives a bit less than four percent of total income. About 40 million Americans lived in poverty in 1960. About 40 million U.S. citizens *still* live in poverty, despite the expenditure of hundreds of billions of dollars in aid for the poor. In the richest country in the world, poverty seems remarkably resilient.

FIRST, THE FACTS

If we are to understand why, we must begin by getting the facts straight. First, even though the *absolute* number of Americans living in poverty has not diminished over the past half-century, population growth has brought a sizable reduction in the *proportion* of Americans who are impoverished. As conventionally measured, more than 22 percent of Americans lived in poverty in 1960. Today, as we emerge from one of the worst recessions of our recent history, about 14 percent of the population is below the official poverty line.

Second, traditional methods of measuring poverty may be misleading because they focus solely on the *cash incomes* of individuals. In effect, government statisticians compute a "minimum adequate" budget for families of various sizes—the "poverty line"—and then determine how many people have cash incomes below this line. Yet major components of the federal government's antipoverty efforts come in the form of **in-kind transfers** (transfers of goods and services, rather than cash) such as Medicare, Medicaid, subsidized housing, food stamps, and school lunches. When the dollar value of these in-kind transfers is included in measures of *total* income, the **standard of living** of persons at lower income levels has improved substantially over the years. There is disagreement over how much of these in-kind transfers should be included in measures of the total income of recipients.[1] Nevertheless, most observers agree that these transfers, plus the **Earned Income Tax Credit** (which gives special **tax rebates** to low-income individuals), are major sources of income for people at the bottom of the income distribution. Adjusting for these transfers and tax credits, it seems likely that over the past fifty years, the proportion of Americans living below the poverty line has been cut roughly in half. Just as important, the real standard of living for the poorest 20 percent of the population has doubled since the mid-1960s. In short, the incidence of poverty in this country has declined markedly over the past half-century, and individuals who remain officially classified as "poor" have a far higher real standard of living than the poor of the 1960s.

THE IMPACT OF INCOME MOBILITY

Whatever measure of income we use, it is crucial to remember that most Americans exhibit a great deal of **income mobility,** tending to move around in the income distribution over time. The most important source of income mobility is the "life-cycle" pattern of earnings. New entrants to the workforce tend to have lower incomes at first, but most workers can enjoy rising incomes as they gain experience on the job. Typically, annual earnings reach a maximum at about age 55. Because peak earnings occur well beyond the **median age** of the population (now about age 37), a "snapshot" of the current distribution of earnings will find most individuals "on the way up" toward a higher position in the income distribution. People who have low earnings now are likely, on average, to have higher earnings in the future.

Another major source of income mobility stems from the operation of Lady Luck. At any point in time, the income of high-income people is likely to be abnormally high (relative to what they can expect on average) due to recent good luck—say, because they just won the lottery or just

---

1 There are two reasons for this disagreement. First, a given dollar amount of in-kind transfers is generally less valuable than the same dollar amount of cash income because cash offers the recipient a greater amount of choice in his or her consumption pattern. Second, medical care is an important in-kind transfer to the poor. Inclusion of all Medicaid expenditures for the poor would imply that the sicker the poor got, the richer they would be. Presumably, a correct measure would include only those medical expenses that the poor would have to incur if they were *not* poor and so had to pay for the medical care (or medical insurance) out of their own pockets.

received a generous bonus. Conversely, the income of people who currently have low incomes is likely to be abnormally low due to recent bad luck—for example, because they are laid up after an automobile accident or have become temporarily unemployed. Over time, the effects of Lady Luck tend to average out across the population. Accordingly, people with high income today will tend to have lower income in the future, while people with low income today will tend to have higher future income. Equivalently, many people living below the poverty line are there temporarily rather than permanently.

The importance of income mobility is strikingly revealed in studies examining the incomes of individuals over time. During the 1970s and 1980s, for example, among the people who were in the top 20 percent (quintile) of income earners at the beginning of the decade, fewer than half were in the top quintile by the end of the decade. Similarly, among the people who were in the bottom quintile at the beginning of the decade, almost half had moved out of that bracket by the end of the decade. Despite news stories that suggest otherwise, income mobility remains robust. From 1996 to 2005 (the decade most recently studied), *more than half* of the people who were in the bottom 20 percent income bracket in 1996 had moved out of that bracket by 2005.

APPEARANCES VERSUS REALITY

Notwithstanding the data just cited, several forces have either increased income inequality in the United States or given the appearance of such an increase, so it is best to be clear about these. Consider first that a rising proportion of the population is *far* above the poverty line. In 1969, for example, about 4 percent of all people in America had earnings six times greater than the poverty-line level. Today, about 6 percent of Americans have earnings that high (above $150,000 for a family of four). Much of this jump in incomes at the top of the income distribution has come at the very top. Thirty years ago, for example, people in the top 10 percent of earners in America pulled in about 31 percent of total income. Today, they garner 37 percent. In even more rarified company, the top 1 percent of earners used to account for 9 percent of total income. Today, they take in 16 percent of income. So even though inflation-adjusted incomes are rising across the board, they appear to be rising the fastest at the very top. Economists are seeking to explain this pattern, which first became apparent during the 1990s. Much work remains to be done, but a few answers are emerging.

First, some key demographic changes are occurring in America. The nation is aging, and an older population tends to have more income inequality than a young population because older people have had more time to experience rising or falling fortunes. Americans are also becoming better educated, and this tends to increase income inequality. People with little education have incomes that tend to cluster together, while the incomes of well-educated people spread out: Some choose to convert their **human capital** into much higher incomes, while others convert it into added leisure time. Taken together, these two demographic changes, aging and education, can account for more than 75 percent of the *appearance* of greater income inequality.

Second, a substantial part of the rapid income growth at the top has really been a matter of accounting fiction rather than reality. Until the late 1980s, there were substantial tax advantages for the very wealthy to have a large portion of their incomes counted as corporate income rather than personal income. In effect, a big chunk of income for the wealthy used to be hidden not from the tax authorities but from the policymakers who worry about the distribution of income. Subsequent changes in the tax laws have since encouraged people to report this income as personal rather than corporate income. Their incomes haven't really changed; it just looks to policymakers like they have.

The third factor we need to account for is the difference in consumption bundles of those near the top of the income distribution and those near the bottom. High-income individuals tend to spend a larger proportion of their incomes on labor-intensive services (such as investment advice, personal care, and domestic help). Low-income individuals tend to spend a larger share of their incomes on nondurable goods, such as food, clothing, shoes, and toiletries. As it turns out, over the past twenty-five years, the items consumed by lower-income individuals have fallen markedly in cost relative to the items consumed by the wealthy. Rising **real wages** have pushed up the costs of service-intensive consumption, while growing international trade with China, India, and other developing nations has pushed down the relative costs of items important to low-income individuals. Overall, this difference in **inflation** rates between the people at the top and those at the bottom of the income distribution has effectively wiped out *all* of the seeming change in their relative incomes over this period.

LIFE AT THE BOTTOM

Nevertheless, it is clear that many people at the bottom of the income distribution are struggling, so we need to take a look at what is going on here. One point is clear: Between 1990 and 2007, the United States experienced a huge influx of immigrants. Newcomers typically earn far less than long-term residents. When large numbers of them are added to the mix of people whose incomes are being measured, *average* income can fall, even when the incomes of all individuals are rising. Thus, immigration has created downward pressure on *measured* incomes at the bottom of the distribution. But new immigrants have also added to competitive pressures in labor markets for less skilled individuals. On balance, it appears that immigration has probably lowered the wages of high school dropouts in America by 4–8 percent. And although this seems small, remember that it is occurring among people whose incomes are already low. Both of these effects are likely to lessen and perhaps even reverse due to the recession of 2007–2009 because deteriorating economic conditions in America caused many recent immigrants to return to their homelands.

Public policy has also taken its toll on the incomes of people at the bottom. The war on drugs, for example, has saddled millions of individuals with criminal records, and the impact has been disproportionately greatest on African Americans, whose incomes were lower to begin with. For example, since 1990, more than two million African American males have served time in jail on serious (felony) drug charges. Once they return to the workforce, they find that their felony records exclude them from a great many jobs—and not just jobs at the top. Often convicted felons cannot find positions that pay more than $8 per hour. The result is that the incomes of such individuals are sharply diminished, which means more poverty.

There is one bright spot on the poverty policy front, however. It is the "welfare reform" program undertaken in 1996. Previously, low-income families had been eligible to receive—for an unlimited duration—federal payments called Aid to Families with Dependent Children (AFDC). The program was converted in 1996 into Temporary Assistance to Needy Families (TANF). Limits were placed on the length of time individuals could receive payments, and all recipients were given additional incentives and assistance to enhance their job skills and to enter or reenter the **labor force.** The full impact of this policy change is still being studied, but it now appears that it has modestly raised incomes among those at the bottom of the income distribution.

Although the resilience of poverty in America is discouraging to the poor and to those who study their plight, it is useful to consider these issues in an international context. In other industrialized nations, such as Japan and most countries in Europe, people at the bottom of the income distribution sometimes (but not always) fare better than the poor in America. Although the poor typically receive a somewhat larger *share* of national income than in America, the national income they share is lower. Hence, compared to America, the poorest 10 percent of the population has a higher average income in Japan and Germany but a lower average income in the United Kingdom and Italy.

In developing nations—which is to say, for the vast majority of people around the world—poverty has a completely different meaning than it does in America. In Africa and much of Asia, for example, it is commonplace for people at the bottom of the income distribution to be living on the equivalent of $400 per *year* or less—in contrast to the $10,000–$15,000 per year they would earn in America. As you saw in Chapter 4, this staggering difference in living standards is due to the vast differences in legal and economic **institutions** that are observed around the world. In America, as in many other industrialized nations, these institutions give people the incentives to put their talents to work and they also protect the fruits of their labors from expropriation by the government. Thus, the best antipoverty program anyone has ever seen is the creation of an institutional environment in which human beings are able to make maximum use of the talents with which they are endowed.

FOR CRITICAL ANALYSIS

1. Why do most modern societies try to reduce poverty? Why don't they do so by simply passing a law that requires that everybody have the same income?

2. How do the "rules of the game" help determine who will be poor and who will not? (*Hint:* How did the Civil Rights Act of 1964, which forbade discrimination on the basis of race, likely affect the incomes of African Americans compared to the incomes of white Americans?) Explain your answer.

3. Which of the following possible in-kind transfers do you think raises the "true" incomes of recipients the most: (a) free golf lessons, (b) free transportation on public buses, or (c) free food? Why?

4. Consider three alternative ways of helping poor people obtain better housing: (a) government-subsidized housing that costs $6,000 per year, (b) a housing **voucher** worth $6,000 per year toward rent on an apartment or a house, or (c) $6,000 per year in cash. Which would you prefer if you were poor? On what grounds might you make your decision?

5. How do government programs that provide benefits for the poor (such as food stamps and subsidized housing) change the incentives of people to be classified as "poor"? Explain.

6. One effect of the **minimum wage** is to reduce employment opportunities for minority teenagers. What effect do you think this has on the long-run poverty rate among minorities? Explain.

CHAPTER 11

Will It Be Inflation
or Deflation?

During the summer of 2008, when gas prices were skyrocketing, the Department of Labor issued a frightening statistic: The **consumer price index (CPI)** had risen more than 5 percent over the prior 12 months, the biggest jump in nearly 20 years. A few months later, the average price of gasoline paid in the United States had dropped from over $4 per gallon to well under $2 per gallon. And as the price of gas was plummeting, **inflation** among primary commodities (such as lumber, metals, and grain) was collapsing as well. As a result, in the late summer and early fall, the overall inflation rate shrank to almost nothing. In fact, during several months in late 2008 and early 2009, overall consumer prices actually *fell*—there was **deflation.** This rapid turn of events quickly switched the Web site and news channel chatter about the problems of inflation into chatter about the prospects for sustained deflation. Before we try to sort out whether inflation or deflation is in your future, let's first make sure we know to what we are referring.

A FORMAL DEFINITION OF
INFLATION AND DEFLATION

Inflation is defined as a rise in the average of all prices, appropriately weighted for their importance in the typical consumer's budget. Inflation is not a change in one price. If the CPI rises by three percent over a 12-month period, what we know is that the appropriately weighted average of prices of goods and services in the United States went up by three percent relative to a year before. (Sometimes you will see references to **core inflation.** This is a measure of the overall change in prices *excluding* energy and food.)

If the rate of change in the **price level** is negative rather than positive, we have deflation—on average, prices are falling rather than rising. As our brief introduction suggests, people worry a lot about inflation, but they also worry about deflation. So we must ask: Are these concerns misplaced?

THE DOWNSIDE OF DEFLATION

Deflation can be troublesome for the economy. One reason is that most of the debts in a modern society like ours are expressed in terms of dollars. When there is deflation, the **real purchasing power** of those dollars goes up. For creditors, this is good news because it means that people now owe them more, measured in terms of the goods and services those dollars will buy (so-called *real* terms). But for debtors, this is bad news, for exactly the same reason. Deflation raises the real burden of the debts they owe. Debtors have to pay back the sums owed with dollars that have a higher purchasing power than the dollars that were lent. In effect, during times of deflation, the inflation-corrected rate of interest (the **real interest rate**) goes up, imposing an added burden on debtors. Although it is possible that deflation's positive effects on creditors and negative effects on debtors could exactly cancel out, often it doesn't happen this way. The result can be significant economic dislocations.

There is also another problem with deflation. It never proceeds evenly and smoothly. During the Great Depression, when prices fell an *average* of about 8 percent per year for four straight years, this deflation did not proceed uniformly over time. Some months and years were worse than others. Moreover, the deflation did not proceed uniformly across all goods. House prices, for example, fell much more than clothing prices. Because of the erratic and unpredictable progression of deflation, individuals and businesses had to focus much of their attention on trying to predict the magnitude and timing of changes in the prices of goods and services. Had there been no deflation, they could have been producing new goods and services instead. The result was that the U.S. economy had fewer goods and services available for **consumption.**

THE COSTS OF INFLATION

Inflation acts as a tax on people's holdings of money—that is, their holdings of **currency** and **checkable deposits.** All of us hold some currency and checkable deposits because of the convenience they provide. As a result, each of us loses **wealth** whenever there is inflation because the purchasing power of our money balances decreases at the rate of inflation.

Assume that you have $20 stashed in your wallet as an emergency cash reserve, that is, you have no immediate expectation of spending it. If at the end of one year there has been a 10 percent rise in the price level, the purchasing power of that $20 note will only be $18, measured in terms of taxi rides or sandwiches. You will have lost value equal to 10 percent times the amount of currency you kept in your wallet.

In essence, then, the purchasing power, or real value, of the money we hold depreciates when there is inflation. The only way we can avoid this type of **inflation tax** on the money we hold is to reduce our holdings of money. But doing this is not an easy matter. It is beneficial—productive—to have money on hand to pay for the things that we want when we want them rather than trying to purchase everything at the beginning of a pay period so as to minimize the dollars in our checkable accounts or in our wallets.

Thus, one cost to society of inflation is that it increases the cost of holding money. For society as a whole, we therefore use *too little* money during periods of inflation. This effect is greatest for currency because its real value falls one-for-one with each rise in the price level. The tax is much less for checkable deposits because many of these accounts pay some interest, and the **nominal interest rate** rises when the expected inflation rate rises.

We should also add that periods of inflation generate exactly the sort of prediction problems that arise when there is deflation. Inflation never proceeds evenly across time or across goods. As a result, during periods of inflation, consumers and businesses must spend some of their time trying to predict exactly how the inflation is likely to proceed. And this in turn means they are spending less time producing output that is available for consumption.

INFLATION, DEFLATION, AND THE MONEY SUPPLY

Throughout the history of the world, there has been a consistent long-run relationship between the change in the price level over time and the change in the **money supply**—money in circulation. This relationship does not move in lockstep fashion in the short run. But it does hold, on average, over longer periods of time, and it is *sustained* inflation or deflation that is a cause for the greatest concern.

There are several ways to define a country's money supply. For our purposes, let's treat it as currency plus all of the funds in accounts that can be used for transactions, such as those accessible with debit cards. As already noted, a predictable long-term relationship has been observed between changes in the money supply and changes in the general price level: sustained, rapid monetary growth yields inflation, and sustained shrinkage in the money supply causes deflation. **Expansive monetary policy** on the part of the **Federal Reserve** caused the money supply to increase quite rapidly after the short **recession** in 2001–2002, for example. The expansion in the money supply continued through the decade. Not surprisingly, inflation crept upward, from 1.6 percent in 2001 to over 4 percent in 2007. And as inflation rose, so did concerns over how bad it would get.

DEFLATION DISCUSSIONS FRONT AND CENTER

The talk of inflation came to a screeching halt at the end of the summer of 2008. Partly it was those plummeting gas and commodity prices that took the steam out of the inflation talk. But the financial panic of 2008 also changed sentiments about the likely course of the future price level.

Indeed, all of Washington, DC, and the financial world suddenly started worrying about deflation. According to Professor Frederic Mishkin of Columbia University, "If inflation expectations were to decline sharply, that would greatly increase the risk of deflation." Further, according to American Enterprise Institute researcher Desmond Lachman, "A deep and prolonged recession could raise the specter of deflation of the sort that plagued the Japanese economy." Lachman was referring to the 1990s, when Japan experienced a flat or declining price level (some economists refer to this as Japan's "lost decade").

Thus far, however, this talk of deflation has not turned out to be reality—and we doubt that it will. Among other things, the Fed reacted to the Panic of '08 with much easier credit policies, injecting more money into the economy. Initially, banks were not very amenable to lending out these new funds, so there were few signs of inflationary pressure in 2009 and 2010. But unless the Fed manages to move these funds out of the system as the economy recovers from the recession, inflationary trouble lies ahead.

So here is our prediction, notwithstanding the dire predictions of falling prices. Inflation is in your future. Eventually, all the increases in the money supply that were made possible by the Fed's credit expansion in 2008–2010 will be realized. As the economy accelerates, banks will be lending their plentiful **excess reserves.** The money supply will be growing, the demand for products will be rising, and the inflation rate will be rising. Thus, our bet is that by the time you read these words, talk of deflation will have stopped because inflation will be a regular part of life once again.

FOR CRITICAL ANALYSIS

1. When the price of a barrel of petroleum increased greatly in 2008, every news article about rising oil prices had a negative slant. When the price of petroleum dropped by more than 50 percent later in the year, the press said little, and much of what the press said was negative. Those negative comments focused on fears that there would not be enough new exploration for oil in the future. Is it really possible for a rise in the price of a good to be "bad" and also for a drop in the price of that same good to be "bad"?

2. If the inflation rate is fully anticipated, what are the ways in which consumers and businesses can protect against the resulting loss of purchasing power?

3. Who are the people who are most affected by unanticipated inflation? Why?

4. Throughout much of 2010, the talk of deflation persisted, even though the price level was rising. It was as though people preferred to live in a world of rising, rather than falling (or even stable), prices. Can you suggest an explanation for people's preferences that there be inflation rather than deflation of stable prices?

5. Between 2008 and 2010 the Federal Reserve doubled the monetary base, which is enough, in the long run, to double the money supply. Given the observed long-run relationship between the money supply and the price level, how much can we expect the price level to rise, ceteris paribus?

6. During 2009 the Fed started paying interest to banks on the reserves they held. The Fed also seemed surprised that the banks then held on to their reserves rather than lending them out. Can you suggest a policy change that would induce the banks to lend out more of their reserves? What would you do if you wanted them to lend out even *fewer* funds to potential borrowers? Explain your answers.

CHAPTER **12**

Is It Real, or Is It Nominal?

Every few years, some important commodity, such as gasoline, electricity, or food, experiences a spike in prices. Reporters examine such price spikes and plaster newspapers, magazines, and Web sites with the appropriate headlines—sometimes relentlessly, day after day. TV commentators interview frustrated and worried Americans who spout the expected negative reactions to the higher prices of essential items in their budgets. The world, it would seem, is coming to an end.

WAS GAS REALLY EXPENSIVE?

Let's just take one often-in-the-press example, gasoline prices. The authors of the book you are reading are old enough to remember the TV interviews that ensued when the price of gas first hit the unprecedented level of $1 per gallon, back in 1980. The same types of interviews occurred when the price of a gallon of gas broke the $2 barrier, early in 2005, and lodged above $3 in 2007. Not surprisingly, virtually the same types of interviews occurred when the price of a gallon of gas rose above $4 in the summer of 2008. At each point in time, everyone interviewed had the same response, even though years had passed between the different price spikes: "I guess I'll just have to stop driving." "I'm going to get a bike." "I'm selling my big car and getting a small one." And of course, each time there was an accompanying story about how record numbers of people were (or soon would be) flocking to their neighborhood motor scooter dealerships.

If we wish to sensibly analyze the effects of higher prices on the quantity demanded and the quantity supplied of any good or service in this world, we can rely neither on what journalists report nor on what

Americans say when they are interviewed. After all, what is important is not what people say but what they do. As economists, we best understand consumers by their **revealed preferences.** Similarly, business people are best understood by their actions, not their words. What people do is reflected in how much they actually buy of any good or service after its price changes, not by their complaints to a TV reporter or what they post on their blog or on Facebook.

Relative Prices, Nominal Prices, and Inflation

For both microeconomic and macroeconomic analysis, the relevant price is the price *relative to* all other prices because people's decisions are based on **relative prices,** not **nominal prices.** The latter simply tell us the number of pieces of paper (dollar bills) you must hand over for a good. Nominal prices tell us nothing about the real sacrifice (measured in terms of other goods or of labor services) that one must make to obtain those goods. Relative prices reflect the real sacrifice involved in acquiring a good because they tell us the price of a good or service relative to the price of another good or service or to the average of all other prices. Relative prices tell us how much of other goods we must sacrifice.

Said another way, we have to separate out the rise in the general price level, called **inflation,** and the rise in the nominal price of a particular good or service. If *all* nominal prices went up exactly 3 percent, there would be no change in relative prices. This inflation of 3 percent would not change the real sacrifice entailed in acquiring any particular good. In the real world, even during periods of inflation, some prices go up faster than others and some prices even go down—witness the price of computing power, DVD players, and MP3 players. Nevertheless, if we want to predict people's behavior, we must know what has happened to the *relative* price of a good, and to determine this, we must adjust for inflation.

Gas Prices Revisited

Now let's get back to our example of gasoline prices. Your grandparents might be able to talk about buying gas for 30 cents a gallon (its average nominal price most of the time between 1956 and 1964). Today, what you pay in dollars per gallon is many times that level. People still drive nonetheless—indeed, the use of gasoline for cars and trucks in the United States is roughly triple what it was when the nominal price of gas was only 30 cents. Something must have happened. The most important "something" is a general rise in *all* prices, including gasoline prices.

In the summer of 2008, the price of gasoline spiked over $4 per gallon. One presidential candidate argued that the government should intervene on gas prices to "give families some relief." Two-thirds of American voters at that time said they thought that the price of gas was "an extremely important political issue." (Of course, when gas prices started tumbling in the fall of 2008, there were not many front-page articles or TV interviews with happy consumers. And the politicians simply became silent on this subject.) Consider, though, that at its nominal price at the beginning of 2009, the *relative* price of gas was back down to about what it had been in 1960—after correcting for overall inflation. For many people, this is a shocking revelation. But correcting for inflation is absolutely essential if you want to sensibly analyze the price of anything over time. Often we talk about the **real price** of a good or service. This refers specifically to subtracting the rate of inflation from the change in a nominal price over time. Not surprisingly, we also do the same exercise when we want to go from **nominal income** to **real income** over time.

THE IMPORTANCE OF HIGHER DISPOSABLE INCOME

Another fact is particularly relevant when thinking about the real burden of gasoline. People are becoming more productive over time because they are getting better educated and because ongoing technological change enables us to produce more with a given input of our time. As a result of this higher **productivity**, U.S. consumers' **disposable incomes** generally rise from one year to the next—and certainly rise on average over longer periods of time. As Americans become richer on average, they are financially able to handle even higher relative prices of those items they wish to purchase, gasoline included.

To help us understand this point better, researchers Indur Goklany and Jerry Taylor came up with an "affordability index." They compared family income to the price of gas from 1949 to 2008. They arbitrarily set 1960 at an affordability index of 1. Relative to this, a higher affordability index number means that something is more affordable. Even when gas was $4.15 per gallon, the affordability gas index was 1.35. In other words, the ratio of the average person's disposable income to the price of gasoline was higher by about 35 percent in 2008 than it was in 1960—gasoline was *more* affordable than it had been back in 1960, when your grandparents were filling up their tanks at 30 cents a gallon. That's hard to believe for some of us but true nonetheless. And once gas prices turned down at the end of 2008, the gas affordability index rose even more, passing 2, meaning that gasoline was more than twice as affordable at the beginning of 2009 as it had been in 1960. A subsequent rise in gas prices meant that by 2011 gas was "only" about 50 percent more affordable than it had been in 1960.

PRODUCT QUALITY CHANGES

The quality of gasoline typically does not change much over time. But the quality of many other products often changes significantly over time, usually for the better. Often we forget about this crucial aspect when we start comparing prices of a good or service over time. If you ask senior citizens today how much they paid for their first car, you might get prices in the range of $2,000–$5,000. The average new car today costs around $30,000 (in nominal dollars). By now, of course, you know that if you want to compare these numbers, you have to first account for the inflation that has occurred over whatever time period you are examining. In this case, adjusting for inflation still means that the relative price of a car appears to be about 50 percent higher than it was, say, fifty years ago.

Does that necessarily mean that a car is really 50 percent more expensive than it was in 1960? Probably not. We must take into account improved quality features of cars today compared to those of the past. Today (unlike fifty years ago), the average car has the following:

- Antilock computer-controlled power brakes
- Power steering
- Digital radio with CD or MP3 player
- Air conditioning
- Steel-belted radial tires
- Cruise control
- Power windows and locks
- Air bags
- Fifty percent better fuel economy

The list of improved and new features is actually much longer. Today, the average car is safer, breaks down less often, needs fewer tune-ups, has a host of amenities that were not even dreamed of fifty years ago, and almost certainly lasts for at least twice as many miles. If you correct not only for inflation but also for these quality increases, the relative price of cars today has almost certainly *fallen* appreciably in the past fifty years, in spite of the "sticker shock" that you may experience when you go shopping for a new car. That is, appearances to the contrary, the inflation-corrected **constant-quality price** of automobiles is actually lower today than it was five decades ago.

DECLINING NOMINAL PRICES

The necessity of adjusting for inflation and quality changes continues to apply even when we are examining goods whose nominal prices have declined over time. A good example is computing power. The nominal price of the average personal computer has gone down in spite of general inflation over the past several decades. These days, a Windows-based desktop computer has an average price of about $500. For a laptop, the average price is a bit over $600. A decade ago, the average machines in each category would have had nominal prices of twice as much. You might be tempted to conclude, then, that the price of personal computing has fallen by 50 percent. You'd be wrong: The price has actually fallen by *more* than 50 percent.

Why? There are two reasons. First, over the past 10 years, the average dollar prices of all goods increased by 30 percent. That is how much overall inflation there has been. That means that the *relative* price of the average computer has fallen by two-thirds, which, of course, is greater than 50 percent. But even here we are missing something extremely important: The quality of what you are buying—computing power—has skyrocketed. The processor speed of the average computer today is at least ten times greater than it was 10 years ago and is increasing exponentially. Moreover, hard drives are bigger, monitors are flatscreen LCDs instead of bulky old cathode ray tubes, laptops are lighter, RAM is larger—the list of improvements goes on and on. And despite people's frustrations with both the hardware and software of the personal computer today, long-time users can tell you that both are vastly more reliable than they were a decade ago. Thus, if you only look at the inflation-corrected decrease in computer prices, you will be underestimating the *true* decrease in the relative price of computers.

The moral of our story is simple. At some point in your education, you learned that "what goes up must come down." Now you know that when it comes to prices, it is often the case that "what goes up has actually gone down." It is a lesson worth keeping in mind if you really want to understand the behavior of consumers and businesses alike.

FOR CRITICAL ANALYSIS

1. Create a list of goods (or services) whose quality has improved over time in such a way that the current prices of these commodities do not accurately reflect their real prices, even after adjusting for inflation. Now see if you can come up with a list of items whose quality has systematically *decreased* over time. Can you suggest why it is easier to find examples of the former than the latter?

2. The demand for small-engine motor scooters jumped when the price of gasoline started moving up in the summer of 2008. Make a prediction about the demand for this form of transportation in, say, two years from today. Explain your answer.

3. Explain why you will make more accurate predictions if you focus on the changing incentives people face rather than listening to what they say they are going to do.

4. When the price of gasoline rose to $4 from $2 per gallon, media commentators spoke as though people were headed to the poor house as a result. But here are some other facts: The average car is driven about 12,000 miles per year and gets about 24 miles per gallon. Even if people did not drive less when the price of rose, by how much did the average driver's "real" income fall due to the $2 per gallon rise in the price of gas? Given that per capita income is almost $50,000 per year, what is this income change in percentage terms? Show all calculations.

5. One implication of the **law of demand** is that the pain to a consumer of a price increase is always *less* than suggested by multiplying the price increase by the amount of the product consumed before the price increase. Explain why.

6. The law of demand also implies that the pleasure that comes from a fall in the price of a good is always *more* than implied by simply multiplying the price cut by the amount of the good consumed before the change. Explain why.

PART THREE

Fiscal Policy

CHAPTER 13

Are You
Stimulated Yet?

George Bush supported one. Barack Obama proposed one too. And Republicans and Democrats in both houses of Congress ended up passing two of them. With all of this backing, surely economic stimulus packages must be good for the economy, right? Well, maybe not. Let's see why.

Stimulus Packages

As implemented by the U.S. (or foreign) governments, so-called economic stimulus packages generally contain some combination of two elements: higher government spending and lower government taxes. One consequence of such packages is that the size of the government **deficit** grows, implying that the **national debt** must get larger. Higher debt is merely a side effect of a stimulus package, however. The *objective* of such packages is to increase total spending in the economy, raise employment, and reduce the unemployment rate.

Proposals for stimulus packages generally come during economic recessions, when gross domestic product (GDP) is depressed and the unemployment rate is elevated. At first blush, it seems like a government stimulus is exactly what we need at such times. After all, government spending is part of GDP, so more government spending seemingly must, as a matter of definition, generate more GDP. And because the things that the government buys (such as cement for new highways) are produced using labor, it seems pretty clear that more people will be hired, thereby cutting the unemployment rate. Alternatively, to the extent that part of the stimulus comes in the form of a tax cut, this puts more **disposable income** in the hands of consumers, some or all of which will presumably be spent by them. Again, production of goods and services rises and the unemployment rate falls. Either way, it seems, a government stimulus package is the sure-fire way out of a recession. Before we jump to this conclusion, however, it will be wise to take a closer look.

TAX CUTS

Let's look first at the tax cuts that are often components of stimulus packages. To do so, imagine for the moment that we keep government spending at current levels and simply cut the taxes we are collecting from people during the current period. Such an action is what people have in mind when they refer to a "tax cut." To fully appreciate the effects of a tax cut, however, we must carefully specify how it is conducted. For example, in the "Economic Stimulus Act of 2008" the tax cut consisted of **lump sum tax rebates.** Each eligible person received $300, regardless of income, with another $300 for each dependent child.[1] In contrast, tax cuts pushed by Presidents Kennedy in the 1960s, Reagan in the 1980s, or Bush in the early 2000s reduced the **marginal tax rate** for many taxpayers. That is, the taxes taken out of additional dollars of earned income were reduced. This not only lowered the individual's **tax liability** (total taxes owed) it also increased the incentive to work more, produce more, and thus earn more, because taxpayers could keep more of what they earned.

However the tax cut is implemented, it is clear that if the government is going to pay for its spending, at least initially it must borrow, that is, run a budget deficit. Now, unless potential lenders are convinced they will be repaid, they will not lend. And the only way for the government to repay its loans is to collect *more* taxes in the future, indeed taxes that are higher by enough to repay both the principle and the interest on the loan.

Now we see the problem with trying to stimulate the economy by cutting taxes: A reduction in *current* taxes must be met by an even larger increase in *future* taxes. For a given level of government spending, taxes *cannot* actually be reduced, they can at best only be moved around in time. Thus, although a "tax cut" puts more current disposable spending in the hands of consumers, it also loads them up with an even bigger added debt burden. In the case of tax cuts of the rebate variety, this is the end of the story. The added debt burden will weigh on the spending decisions of consumers, so there is no necessary reason to think

---

1 For individuals earning over $75,000 or couples earning over $150,000 the rebate was gradually phased out to zero, and thus technically not lump sum. This actually tended to discourage some work effort among these individuals, which would tend to *reduce* real GDP. This effect was likely quite small, however, because the dollar amounts were small.

that consumers will spend more today. They may (and typically do) just save most of the increase in disposable income so they'll be ready in the future when their bigger tax bills come due. Of course, consumers may not *think* this way about their taxes at all. But the key point is how they *behave*. And the fact is that many consumers act *as though* they are quite conscious of the added burden of future taxes they bear when current taxes are cut. Hence, tax rebates such as contained in the Economic Stimulus Act of 2008 typically cannot do much to stimulate the economy in any important way.

Reductions in marginal tax rates offer hope of something more. Again, we cannot expect people to go on a spending spree just because taxes have been moved around in time. But there is an added feature with lower marginal tax rates. People have an incentive to work more, produce more, and thus earn more, because they get to keep a larger share of what they earn. This feature of this type of tax cut does indeed stimulate the economy, although it does so from the supply side (labor supply rises), rather than the demand side.

Spending Increases

Now, what about the other half of stimulus packages—higher spending by the government? To sort this out, we will first have to distinguish between two broad types of government spending: that which is a substitute for private spending and that which is not. For example, although the government spends plenty on education (primary, secondary, and college), so do private citizens. The government spending is a substitute for private spending, and when the government spends more on education, private spending on education falls. This offsetting change in private spending clearly reduces the potential stimulus effect of the government. Indeed, in some cases, education included, it appears that *all* of the higher government spending is offset by lower private spending. The stimulus effect in this case is obviously zero.

Of course, plenty of government programs don't compete directly with private spending. For example, most defense spending (such as expenditures on the war in Afghanistan) does not compete with private spending. Also, some so-called infrastructure spending, such as on highways and bridges, competes little with private spending. Thus, when government defense or infrastructure spending goes up, there is no direct dollar-for-dollar cut in private spending, as there can be with items like education. Nevertheless, there are generally substantial *indirect* impacts on private spending—impacts that can markedly reduce the stimulating effects of the government spending. Let's see why.

INDIRECT OFFSETS IN PRIVATE SPENDING

As we suggested above, the real burden of the government is its spending. Taxes are simply the means of deciding who shall bear that burden. Thus, for a given level of other expenditures, when defense or infrastructure spending rises, taxes *must* rise, at some point now or in the future. And because consumers know this, they will typically make some provision for it, by reducing their own spending. This clearly dampens the overall stimulus effect of the higher government spending.

There is another potential offset when government spending rises. If the government "finances" this spending by borrowing rather than raising current taxes, the result can be upward pressure on interest rates. Higher interest rates in turn reduce the attractiveness of consumer durable goods (such as houses and cars) and also reduce the profitability of business investment spending. Thus, when larger government deficits push up interest rates, private consumption and investment spending will decline, once more dampening any hoped-for stimulus.

DELAYS IN SPENDING

As amazing as this may seem, there is yet one more obstacle in the path of stimulus spending—time. Despite all the headlines about so-called "shovel ready" projects and "immediate action," there are usually long delays in implementing the spending portion of stimulus packages. Let's consider one simple example. As part of the 2009 stimulus pushed by President Obama and passed by Congress early in that year, more than a dozen states were supposed to get federal funds for building or expanding light rail commuter systems. Ultimately, two of the states (Wisconsin and Ohio) decided that the benefits of this spending to them would not outweigh the costs. Hence, these states declined to accept the money for light rail systems, hoping the federal government would let them keep the money and use it to repair and expand their roads and bridges. In fact, late in 2010 (nearly two years after the stimulus package was passed) President Obama ordered that the rejected funds be redirected to the dozen states that had accepted the rail funding. Well into 2011 most of these funds were still unspent, as were many billions of dollars of other funds included in the "2009" stimulus package.

Not all spending is delayed this much, of course (although some can be delayed even more). But the key point is simple. Despite all of the claims politicians make about taking "immediate action," it just doesn't work out this way. In fact, over the span of the last fifty years or so, much of the government spending supposedly designed to help pull us out of recessions was not actually spent until well after these recessions were over.

The Stimulus that Mostly Wasn't

The 2009 American Recovery and Reinvestment Act (ARRA), President Obama's first major piece of legislation, received lots of media attention, in no small part because of its size—$862 billion. But its impact on aggregate demand appears to have been minimal. One reason stems from the fact that a large portion of the legislation called for grants to state and local governments. The law's backers argued that these funds would immediately be spent by the recipients on all sorts of new programs, thereby stimulating the economy. In fact, the state and local governments used almost *all* of these transfers to reduce their borrowing. Thus, the mechanics went like this: the federal government borrowed funds (about $120 billion per year during each of the first two years), lent those funds to the states, which then borrowed $120 billion less. Net effect: federal debt up, state and local debt down, and aggregate spending unchanged.

The ARRA was also touted as being big on infrastructure—roads, bridges, and so forth. In fact, the legislation itself never called for more than about 10 percent of its funds to be used in this way, and by two years after its passage, only a small fraction of this had been spent. Indeed, the ARRA appears to have yielded almost no increase in government spending on goods and services, at least through 2010. Twenty-one months into the act's existence, government purchases of goods and services had risen only $24 billion, and infrastructure had gone up only $3 billion. In a $14 trillion economy, these sums are trivial.

Is Stimulus Possible?

As you may have gathered, our overall conclusion is that, unless marginal tax rates are reduced, we should typically not expect government stimulus packages to actually stimulate the economy very much. Lump sum tax cuts are not really tax cuts at all, and higher government spending levels are routinely offset in whole or in part by cuts in private spending. But notice our use of the word "typically." There is indeed a set of circumstances in which stimulus packages have the potential to live up to their billing. Fortunately, these circumstances don't come around very often. Indeed, the only time they may have been observed is during and immediately after the Great Depression (1929–1933).

A series of declines in aggregate demand over the period 1929–1933 ended up pushing economy-wide output down by 30 percent and raising the unemployment rate to an unprecedented 25 percent of the labor force. By the depths of 1933, many people had been unemployed for years and they and their families were living hand to mouth. They were

cash-constrained. Every time their income changed by a dollar, so too did their spending. Thus, when so-called "relief" spending by the federal government began, most people worried not a bit about the future tax liabilities that might be involved. Moreover, much of the spending was on items (such as the Hoover Dam, and Post Office and other public buildings) that did not compete directly with private spending.

This set of circumstances meant that the government stimulus spending during the 1930s did help increase total spending and also helped get people back to work. Indeed, it was during this period of time that stimulus spending first gained credibility among both economists and politicians. But the circumstances of the 1930s were extreme. No recession since then has come remotely close to being as severe, not even the recessions of 1981–1982 and 2007–2009. Moreover, since the 1930s credit markets have become much more developed. People have credit cards and lines of credit and thus the ability to continue spending even when their incomes decline. To be sure, a prolonged period of unemployment can eventually exhaust these reserves. Fortunately, the number of people who find themselves in such circumstances is generally small, even in recessions. As a result, the stimulating effects observed for stimulus packages during the 1930s cannot be expected to be repeated, unless of course the 1930s somehow repeat themselves.

So our moral is that if you are not yet feeling stimulated by federal spending increases or tax cuts, don't feel left out. You have plenty of company.

FOR CRITICAL ANALYSIS

1. Why is it in the interest of politicians to promote the notion that unemployment can be lowered if federal spending is increased?

2. If the unemployment rate can be reduced by cutting taxes, why don't we cut taxes to zero, at least during recessions?

3. During World War II, federal spending rose to roughly 50 percent of total spending in the economy, from its prewar level of just under 10 percent. How was this possible—that is, what spending had to decline to make it feasible for the federal share of spending to rise by a factor of five?

4. Some people argue that unemployment benefits (i.e., cash payments by the government to people who are unemployed) help stimulate the economy. The reasoning is that without the benefits the incomes of unemployed people would be lower, and thus their spending on goods and services would be lower. Keeping in mind that unemployment

benefits are generally no more than 40–50 percent as large as the typical earnings of people when working, answer these questions:

(a) How do unemployment benefits change the incentive to be *employed*? Explain.

(b) Is it possible that a system of unemployment benefits could actually cause total spending in the economy to *fall*? Explain.

5. If current taxes are reduced by way of a lump sum rebate, does the consumer response likely depend on how long it will be before taxes are actually raised to pay off the debt incurred by the government? In answering, be sure to account for the fact that the longer the delay in raising taxes, the greater will be the interest debt that accrues.

6. Who is more likely to think of a cut in current taxes as being a true reduction in taxes: a young worker with several young children or an older retiree with no children? Explain.

CHAPTER 14

Health Care Reform

The trite but true saying "Nothing is more important than your health" should be replaced these days with another: "Nothing is more important than who pays for health insurance and health care." The most massive change in the history of our nation's health care insurance and delivery systems occurred in 2010 with the passage of health care "reform." The stakes are big. Americans spend 17 percent of total national annual income on health care—we are, indeed, the world's health-care spending champions.

HOW ABOUT THE UNINSURED?

So what about all those people who are said to be shut off from this health care system because they lack health insurance? The typical claim in the debate over health care reform was that 15 percent of Americans lacked coverage—but like many numbers you hear in political debates, this one needs to be taken with a grain (or perhaps a shaker) of salt. Of the forty-five million people said to lack health coverage in America, about eighteen million were aged 18–34, a group for which health expenditures are far lower than average. About twelve million were fully eligible for publicly provided (and paid-for) health insurance, but chose not to take it. And among all of the uninsured, fully half were uninsured only part of each year. The bottom line is that only about 3 percent of Americans (fewer than one in thirty) were likely to have a significant demand for health insurance and yet be unable to get insurance on a persistent basis. For these individuals, the lack of insurance was an onerous, often terrifying, fact of life. But it is important to keep in mind that the number of people in this group is a far cry from the numbers that are normally bandied about.

Rising Health Care Costs in America

Fifty years ago, spending on health care in this country was not even 6 percent of national income. Today it is 17 percent, about equally divided between public spending and private spending. And there is no doubt that even as we speak, health care costs have been rising in America. There are at least four reasons why health care costs have gone up so much:

1. *An aging population:* The top 5 percent of health care users incur more than 50 percent of all health care costs. Senior citizens (all of them covered by Medicare) make up most of the top users. It is not surprising, therefore, that as our population ages, we will be spending more on health care. Currently, about 13 percent of U.S. residents are over 65. By 2035, this number will have risen to 22 percent. Given that the elderly consume in excess of four times as much per capita health care services as the rest of the population, the demand for such services is certain to go up with our aging population.

   Of course, populations in Western Europe, Canada, Japan, and other industrialized nations are rising as well. But there the elderly have not played as big a role in pushing up health care costs as in America. The reason is simple. In those other nations, which have national health insurance systems, the elderly are sharply limited on the amount of health care they are allowed to utilize. This is much different from the U.S. Medicare system, which effectively lets senior citizens choose to have whatever health care services they wish.

2. *More expensive technologies:* Each advance in medical technology brings with it more expensive equipment and prescription drugs. A magnetic resonance imaging (MRI) scanner costs at least $2 million. A positron emission tomography (PET) scanner costs over $4 million. Each time these machines are used, the fees range to as high as $2,000 per procedure. New drugs for cancer can easily cost $250,000 for one course of treatment. Innovation in medicine has played a key role in improving the quality of health care in America, and neither innovation nor spending on it is about to stop. Therefore, we can expect increasing expenditures in medicine just because of advances in equipment and drugs.

3. *When someone else pays:* Between the government (through **Medicare** and **Medicaid**) and insurance companies, more than 80 percent of health care spending is paid for by someone else—a **third party.** Less than 20 percent is paid directly by individuals. This was not always the situation. In 1930, third parties paid only about 4 percent of health care expenditures.

When someone else pays for medical services, we encounter the problem of **moral hazard:** Payment by third parties creates a larger quantity demanded. You may think that people do not react to the price of medical services, but they do. When Medicare went into effect in 1965, the volume of federal government–reimbursed medical services increased by more than 65 percent above what was anticipated when the program was made into law. And when senior citizens received new coverage for prescription medicines in 2003, their spending on prescriptions ended up being *double* the forecast.

Consider an example: If you have a health insurance policy that pays everything, then you have little incentive to reduce your medical care purchases. Why not see a doctor about every sniffle "just in case"? If, in contrast, you have to pay the first $1,000 out of your pocket before an insurance company (or the government) will start paying for your medical care expenses, you will react differently. You will engage, at a minimum, in more wellness activities and you will be less inclined to seek medical care for minor problems. Physicians in hospitals face a type of moral hazard problem, too. If they are reimbursed for every procedure by an insurance company or by the government, they will tend to ask for more tests and procedures "just in case." That means we pay more for medical care.

4. *Obesity:* The Centers for Disease Control and Prevention (CDC) have estimated that almost one-third of Americans are obese. In contrast, fifty years ago obesity was a rarity. The CDC estimates that today about 10 percent of total U.S. medical expenditures are attributable to obesity. About half of these expenditures are being paid for by Medicare and Medicaid. Many expenditures for obese people relate to obesity-caused type 2 diabetes—a disease that is rising at a record rate in the United States. As obesity rises, spending on medical care will follow. (For the causes of increased obesity, see Chapter 3.)

HEALTH CARE REFORM TO THE RESCUE?

A bitterly fought battle over the health care system occurred in the U.S. Congress until new health care legislation was signed into law by President Obama in 2010. After briefly reviewing the key aspects of the two-thousand-plus pages of the new law on this matter, you will see that not all of the promised results can actually come to fruition, especially the promise that "spiraling health care costs will come down."

Here is a brief point-by-point summary of the federal government's new national health care program:

1. *Health care regulations*—Health insurance companies must cover everyone who applies, including those with preexisting medical problems. (As explained below, this new rule will weigh heavily (and expensively) on young people.)

2. *Individual mandate*—Just about everyone living in the United States must either purchase health care coverage or pay a fine up to $750 per year for an individual or $2,250 per year per family (twenty-one states have challenged this mandate in federal court).

3. *Employer mandate*—Firms with more than 50 employees must offer health insurance coverage or pay an annual fine of up to $750 per employee who obtains federal subsidies for such coverage.

4. *Health care insurance subsidies*—A variety of subsidies and tax credits will be provided to lower-income people and smaller firms.

5. *Higher taxes*—A special tax rate of 3.8 percent will apply to nearly all income earnings above $200,000 for individuals and $250,000 for a married couple.

THE MORAL HAZARD PROBLEM WILL WORSEN

You have already been introduced to the moral hazard problem that arises when third parties pay for medical care. Health care reform will worsen moral hazard. Once the national health care program fully goes into effect, tens of millions of U.S. residents are going to be paying a smaller percentage of their health care expenses themselves than they did previously. Consequently, the direct price paid by them for health care services will fall and thus the quantity of health care services demanded will rise. Also, because health insurers will be required to cover this expanded consumption of medical services, total expenditures on health care will increase even faster.

Finally, the moral hazard problem will become worse because more U.S. residents will face reduced incentives to make decisions that promote better health. As people have more health problems as a consequence of this increase in moral hazard, the demand for health care will increase. And as you know, when demand rises, so too will prices and expenditures.

WHY YOUNG PEOPLE WILL PAY MORE

The new law means that soon everyone must buy health insurance. The law also states that insurance companies must give full coverage to those with preexisting illnesses, but without charging them a higher rate. What does that mean? Simply that healthy young people—who will be required to buy insurance policies—will not pay a low price that reflects the low risk of them getting sick. One analysis conducted for the *Associated Press* estimates that beginning in 2014 young adults seeking coverage in the individual health insurance market will pay almost 20 percent more for the same coverage that they could buy today. To see why this is likely to be an understated impact of the new rules, consider this fact: Typically, insurance companies have charged six or seven times as much to older customers as to younger ones in those states that had no restrictions. The new federal law limits this ratio to three to one. That means that a 60-year-old can be charged only three times as much as a 25-year-old. So, who gets stuck? Young adults will, in the form of higher premiums.

WON'T EXTRA PREVENTIVE CARE
CUT HEALTH CARE SPENDING?

Supporters of health care reform argue that it will encourage a lot more preventive care, thereby reducing overall health care spending. But Stanford University Medical Professor Abraham Verghese argues that spending more on preventive care will actually drive costs *up*, not down. First of all, everyone knows what illness prevention strategies we can do as individuals—lose weight, eat better, exercise more, smoke less, and wear a seat belt while driving a car. These are cheap, save lives, and cut health care costs.

All other preventive strategies end up costing the economy more. Increased medical screening leads to discovering more potential medical problems and therefore more expenses in the form of additional screening tests and medications. Professor Verghese uses the following example. A test that discovers high cholesterol in a person who is feeling fine is really the discovery of a risk factor and not a disease. Elevated cholesterol levels mean that you have a greater chance of having a heart attack. You could reduce your cholesterol levels through weight loss, better diet, and lots of exercise. Or, you can take a pill every day in the form of a drug called a statin. That pill will reduce your cholesterol levels. Using a statin in the general population costs about $150,000 for every *year* of life it saves in men and costs even more in women. Sorry, no savings to be found here.

THERE ARE INDEED NO FREE LUNCHES

From the onset, the health care debate was couched in absurd contradictions, at least for those who understand limited resources versus unlimited wants, **budget constraints,** and supply and demand. No legislation that promises to subsidize tens of millions of U.S. residents who currently have no health care insurance can possibly lead to lower overall medical care expenditures. That does not mean that such legislation is wrong—that's a value judgment and not a conclusion arising from economic analysis. Nevertheless, it is past time that everyone who takes place in the discussion of health care acknowledges one simple fact. Throughout all recorded history, when any good or service becomes cheaper to the person who uses that good or service, quantity demanded will rise, no matter what the political arguments are to the contrary.

THE MACROECONOMIC EFFECTS OF HEALTH CARE REFORM

Let there be no doubt about it—the most recent health care reform legislation is going to impact the rest of the U.S. economy in significant ways. It will have effects on labor markets, markets for goods and services, and the budgets of federal and state governments. Let's consider these effects in order:

1. *Labor market effects*—The new legislation requires many firms to provide health care insurance when they are currently not providing it. The result will be an increase in the effective wage rates that these firms must pay for each unit of labor. The increased effective wage rate will induce firms to reduce the quantity of labor demanded. The result: Other things being equal, U.S. employment will be lower than it otherwise would have been had there been no mandate requiring firms to pay for employee health care coverage.

2. *Markets for goods and services*—The increase in labor costs that firms will incur in hiring each unit of labor will clearly increase average and marginal costs of production. This will induce firms to decrease their output in all prices. The result: Other things being equal, equilibrium prices will rise in a number of markets and consumers will pay higher prices for many goods and services.

3. *The impact on government budgets*—The new taxes for higher-income people mentioned on page XX went into effect in 2011, so tax revenues began flowing into the new federal health care program immediately. Because federal government expenditures on this new

program are being phased in gradually, the program initially will be financed by the revenues collected in advance. According to most experts, though, the new tax revenues will be insufficient to cover the increases in government health care spending that is going to occur in future years. Ultimately, the federal government will have to search for additional ways to reduce its health care expenditures— such as **price controls** on hospitals and physicians—or increases in tax rates and new taxes. Note that the federal program does not include revenues for states to cover the higher expenses of additional people admitted to the Medicaid program, which state governments administer. Consequently, state governments will also face pressures to increase tax rates or to reduce health care service costs.

For Critical Analysis

1. Is it correct to apply standard economic analysis to something as important as medical care? Why or why not?

2. What are some of the ways in which government could force individuals to undertake their own illness-preventing activities?

3. If the government attempts to reduce health care expenditures by lowering the fees that physicians can charge for certain procedures, what might be the result in the short run? In the long run?

4. Why don't most current health care insurance plans cover preexisting illnesses? Who benefits from this current general rule? When health care reform legislation abolishes this rule, who will be hurt?

5. Currently, most U.S. residents cannot buy health care insurance coverage from a company based in another state. The new legislation leaves this restriction in place. Who benefits from this situation? Who loses?

6. What is special about health care that justifies so much government intervention? In other words, what problems would arise if the health care sector were completely unregulated and unsubsidized?

CHAPTER **15**

The Fannie Mae, Freddie Mac Flimflam

Between 1995 and 2010, the U.S. housing market went on the wildest ride in its history. Over the years 1995–2005, median real (inflation-adjusted) house prices soared 60 percent nationwide and then promptly crashed, falling 40 percent from 2006 to 2010. Over the same period, the proportion of Americans who owned homes, normally a variable that changes quite slowly, leapt from 64 percent to 69 percent and then quickly dropped back to 67 percent. Meanwhile, the number of new houses built each year soared from 1.4 million to 2 million and then plunged to 500,000 per year.

But what really got people's attention—and created huge pressures on financial markets here and abroad—was the fact that just as quickly as people had snapped up houses during the boom years of 1995–2005, they simply *abandoned* their houses beginning in 2006, refusing to make any more payments on their mortgages. In a typical year, about 0.3 percent of homeowners (fewer than one out of three hundred) stop making mort-gage payments and thus have their houses go into foreclosure, a process in which the borrower must give up any **equity** (ownership) in a home because of a failure to meet payment obligations. The foreclosure rate doubled to 0.6 percent in 2006, doubled again in 2007, and rose yet again in 2008, 2009, and 2010. In some hard-hit states, such as Nevada, fore-closures exploded to more than *ten times* the normal nationwide rate, with one home out of thirty going into foreclosure each year.

Across the country, people were literally walking away from their homes, leaving them in the hands of banks and other lenders. These lenders then took huge financial losses when forced to sell the aban-doned properties in a market in which house prices were already falling. The result was further downward pressure on prices, which gave more owners the incentive to walk away from their homes, which raised foreclosures, and so forth. Within just a few years, the housing market was more depressed than it had been at any time since the Great Depression of the 1930s. In fact, to see what happened, we need to go back and start our story during that very period.

SOME HOUSING HISTORY

Prior to World War II, most home mortgages were of short duration, such as one or two years (rather than fifteen to thirty years, which is common now). During the Great Depression, many risk-weary lenders refused to renew mortgages when they came due. The state of the economy was such that most borrowers were unable to repay immediately, and so their homes were foreclosed. In response, the U.S. government in 1934 created the Federal Housing Administration (FHA), to guarantee some home mortgages from default, and in 1938 created the Federal National Mortgage Association (FNMA, known as Fannie Mae), to purchase mortgages from the FHA, enabling the latter to guarantee still more mortgages. In 1968, Congress authorized Fannie Mae to buy mortgages from virtually all lenders, and it also created Ginnie Mae (the Government National Mortgage Association), authorized to bundle up, guarantee, and sell home mortgages issued by the FHA. Two years later, in 1970, Congress created Freddie Mac (the Federal Home Mortgage Loan Corporation) to offer competition to Fannie Mae. Both Fannie Mae and Freddie Mac are referred to as **government-sponsored enterprises (GSEs)**. They are technically independent of the federal government, but both are subject to congressional oversight and, it turns out, to political pressure to do what Congress wants them to do. Ginnie Mae is part of the U.S. Department of Housing and Urban Development and thus under the direct budgetary control of Congress.

It has been clear from the inception of each of these agencies that the intent of Congress has been to promote home ownership in the United States, especially among lower-income individuals. Ultimately, the only way to do this is to reduce costs for borrowers. The agencies have done this in a variety of ways, including allowing people to make down payments of as little as 3.5 percent of the value of the house, as opposed to the 10–20 percent required by private lenders.

Going back as far as 1993, Fannie and Freddie have taken special measures to subsidize the highest-risk borrowers, along the way racking up huge potential risks. But beginning soon after the recession of 2001, Congress made it clear to Fannie, Freddie, Ginnie, and the FHA that even more should be done. In fact, powerful Democratic Representative Barney

Frank explicitly told the agencies that they needed to "roll the dice" in the housing market, that is, take on more risk by insuring, guaranteeing, or making home mortgage loans to people who were much worse credit risks than normal. The organizations responded with enthusiasm, helping to spark the housing boom that finally ended up crashing. Two things made the outcome of this behavior singularly costly. First, at the behest of Congress, the agencies focused most of their efforts on subsidizing purchases by the least creditworthy customers. Second, when it became apparent just how extensive the foreclosure losses were going to be, Congress not only bailed out the agencies by giving them more taxpayer cash but also told them to continue doing more of the same. The result will be huge tax bills for you.

Rolling the Dice

The two riskiest types of mortgages are called subprime and Alt-A, respectively. Subprime mortgages are those made to borrowers who are considered to have a much higher than normal risk of defaulting. These people have relatively poor credit scores and the size of the mortgage they are getting is high relative to their ability to repay. Alt-A mortgages are generally those that either are missing some key documentation (such as proof of the borrower's income) or have especially low down payments. Either way, Alt-A mortgages are riskier than the typical mortgage.

By 2008, Fannie Mae and Freddie Mac either owned or were guaranteeing nearly ten million subprime and Alt-A mortgages. The outstanding balance on these loans was $1.6 *trillion*, a potential liability of $8,000 for each U.S. taxpayer. What made this worse, however, is that since the early 1990s Fannie and Freddie had routinely misrepresented just how risky their portfolios were becoming, reporting that their subprime and Alt-A mortgages were "prime" mortgages (the highest quality, least risky category).

Bailouts

As we saw, both Fannie and Freddie were established as GSEs, that is, privately owned, but publicly sponsored, or endorsed. Although the federal government did not formally guarantee either organization, many people regarded such a guarantee as being implicit. And indeed, when it became apparent in September 2008 that both organizations were **insolvent** (their liabilities exceeded their assets), that implicit guarantee became reality. The federal government initially offered up $200 billion in explicit guarantees. Since then, the size of the guarantee—many people refer to it as a bailout—has been increased twice. Most recently, the Obama administration announced that there was *no limit* on how much the federal government was willing to invest in Fannie and Freddie. Although the Congressional Budget office claims that the cost to taxpayers is likely to be "only" $389 billion, potentially the taxpayer liability is many trillions of dollars.

At this point, you might think that Fannie and Freddie would change their behavior, perhaps by turning to lower-risk loans, or even trying to clean up their balance sheets by getting rid of the worst loans. In fact, both agencies have done just the reverse, getting involved in even riskier loans, and helping borrowers avoid their debts at little or no cost to the borrowers. The result is that the likely cost to taxpayers continues to rise.

CASH UNLIMITED

As a practical matter, Fannie Mae and Freddie Mac have gotten themselves involved in almost every nook and cranny of the U.S. housing market. Consider just two examples. First, plenty of people in the housing market are either "underwater" (the value of their home is less than what is owed on it) or simply unable or unwilling to continue making payments on the mortgage. Fannie and Freddie have been actively engaged in a loan forgiveness program for many of these people, although this is not what the program is called. Essentially, the two agencies have been purchasing existing mortgages that are in default and then "modifying" them by reducing the amount the borrower owes. Rather than reporting this as a debt forgiveness (something that likely would not set well with homeowners who are still paying their bills), Fannie and Freddie just report the forgiveness as a "credit-related expense."

Of course, some people just cannot or will not continue making payments, even when offered a substantial reduction in the amount of the mortgage. In these cases, Fannie and Freddie have been taking over ownership of the homes—at a rate of one every ninety seconds. By 2010 the two agencies owned 170,000 homes, more houses than are located in Seattle. After putting still more cash into the properties (about $10,000 per house) to ready them for sale, the agencies then hand them over to real estate agents to sell for whatever price they can get—which of course is always far below what was owed on them. And the borrowers? Well, they are off the hook, replaced by the taxpayers.

IT MAY GET WORSE

The meltdown in housing markets slowed the issuance of new mortgages by banks, and thus slowed the growth of Fannie and Freddie. While this may help reduce future losses by these two organizations, it won't stem the overall flood of losses. Why not? It's simple. The FHA has dramatically *increased* the amount of lending it is undertaking, and as a practical matter virtually all FHA loans are made to borrowers who are riskier than average. Moreover, the risks of FHA loans are enhanced by the fact that it requires a down payment of only 3.5 percent of the value of the home. Some experts now believe that up to one in ten of all FHA loans will end up in default—which means that taxpayers will be footing the bill.

Just how costly the federal involvement in mortgage markets will become is anyone's guess. In the meantime, the federal government seems determined to keep the cash flowing, which means that your tax bill will keep on growing. How high it will go, no one knows.

For Critical Analysis

1. Who benefits from the actions of Fannie and Freddie?

2. There are approximately 220 million taxpayers in the United States, at least as measured by the number of tax returns filed with the IRS. But only about half of these "taxpayers" end up paying income taxes. (Some of the others pay only Social Security or Medicare taxes, while some actually *receive* payments, under the Earned Income Tax Credit program.) Considering that Fannie and Freddie are now owners or guarantors of almost $5.5 trillion in mortgages, what is the maximum potential liability for each of the taxpayers who actually pay income taxes?

3. How does the FHA requirement of a low down payment affect the incentive of the borrower to default on his or her mortgage, that is, stop making the payments? What impact does this have on taxpayer liability for these loans? Explain.

4. What characteristics of the people in a congressional district would help explain whether the member of Congress representing that district favored or opposed the actions of Fannie Mae and Freddie Mac? Explain.

5. Why do low-income and high-risk borrowers receive subsidies from Fannie, Freddie, Ginnie, and FHA? Make sure you address the question of why doesn't the government simply hand them cash every year, rather than subsidizing their purchases of houses.

6. Given the huge losses incurred by Fannie and Freddie as a result of "rolling the dice," why do you suppose Congressman Barney Frank hasn't been voted out of office?

CHAPTER 16

Big Bucks
for Bailouts

Alstom, American International Group (AIG), Anglo Irish Bank, Bear Stearns, Citigroup, General Motors (GM), Chrysler, Freddie Mac, and Fannie Mae. What do these companies—which are based in a variety of nations and offer different products—all have in common? They have been "saved" by government (read: taxpayer) subsidies. They were, according to proponents of these subsidies, just "too big to fail." Now that concept—too big to fail—could be looked at in the alternative. Perhaps those companies were too big to save—at least from the points of view of taxpayers and the long-run efficiency of each country's economy. We shall first look at what "too big to fail" means, and then examine this concept in the context of what has been called **industrial policy.**

THE LOGIC (OR ILLOGIC) BEHIND
TOO-BIG-TO-FAIL POLICIES

The people who support preventing very large corporations from failure, whether those companies are manufacturers of high-speed trains, insurance providers, investment banks, commercial banks, automobile producers, or large guarantors of mortgages, sincerely believe that a failure of a very large corporation can create **systemic risk,** that is, threaten a widespread reduction in economic activity throughout an economy.

Consider two contrasting examples. Your local CD retailer is having a tough time competing against online downloads. Eventually, the company goes out of business, laying off its three employees and abandoning the rented retail space in the local mall. There are no systemic risks with such an event. A few people have to look for jobs and the landlord of the rented space has to find another tenant, but that is the extent of the impact of the firm's closure. Now consider GM. For years prior to its partial takeover by the government, it was losing hundreds of millions, even billions, of dollars per year. Over the past half century or so, during good economic times GM routinely agreed to generous labor contracts. During bad economic times, it was stuck with high labor costs, including high pension benefits (see Chapter 17). By the time the recession of 2007–2009 rolled around, GM was simply uncompetitive due to its high costs. Just as the company was about to go under, it was saved by the U.S. government (with subsequent help from the Canadian government). Those who argued for government intervention claimed that GM's bankruptcy would put several hundreds of thousands of people out of work and lead to a vicious cycle of increasing unemployment throughout the United States and elsewhere. In other words, GM was too big to fail and had to be saved. The systemic risks were supposedly too great to let it go under.

THE MORAL HAZARD PROBLEM WITH "SAVING" LARGE CORPORATIONS

When large corporations are "saved" by the government, the taxpayers who actually pay the bill also face the possibility of a **moral hazard** problem. Why? Consider how labor leadership and management in corporations can reason if they believe they are candidates to be "saved." Believing that they will not be allowed to fail, they can engage in activities that are not necessarily in the long-term interests of the company. (And, we should add, not in the interests of the taxpayers (that's you and us) who will be subsidizing them.)

When times are tough, the head of a labor union whose workers produce GM's cars knows that the union does not have to "give back" very much to the company in terms of lowered fringe benefits and lower wages. Why should it? The company is too big to fail, after all. The managers of GM act the same way: They know that during tough times they don't have to institute dramatic cost-saving actions because—you guessed it—GM is too big to fail.

This moral hazard problem influenced the behavior of all of the large corporations that were saved by taxpayers in the United States—Chrysler, Citicorp, Goldman Sachs, and AIG, among others. Those companies' workers and managers were no longer subjected to an unfettered competitive marketplace, and they acted accordingly. The result was (and continues to be) the **inefficient** use of resources. Costs were not trimmed where and when they should have been, excessive risks were assumed, and so forth. As a result, resources were not employed in their most productive uses. So, not only are taxpayers footing the bill, but also the economy will in general grow less rapidly than it would have without the subsidies to the too-big-to-fail corporations.

INDUSTRIAL POLICY IS BACK IN FASHION

The latest worldwide recession officially lasted from 2007 to 2009, but its reverberations may still be going on as you read this. The recession brought back in vogue something called **industrial policy.** The too-big-to-fail policies examined above are just an example of this policy. The way President Barack Obama put it in 2009 was this: The government must make "strategic decisions about strategic industries." The $800 billion stimulus legislation in that year earmarked billions of taxpayer dollars for investment in "strategic" sectors, such as renewable energy, advanced vehicles, and high-speed rail systems. But the United States was not alone. At about the same time, Japan announced that it would create a strategy to make sure that its key industries would not be "left behind." France declared that it would invest in "strategic" industries, too, although the government there used the phrase "national champions." The bottom line is that an essential part of the new industrial policy in Europe and Asia, as in America, has been to lavish taxpayer subsidies on banks, car-makers, and other favored industries.

If we define industrial policy as attempts by governments to promote the growth of particular industrial sectors and companies, history does not shed a favorable light on these policies. Simply claiming, as Obama did when he visited Detroit in 2010, that taxpayer subsidies "saved jobs" does not really tell us anything. After all, the correct analysis of any industrial policy must compare costs with benefits. How much did those "saved" jobs cost the economy?

Consider the example of the semiconductor industry. Japan spent somewhere between $20 and $50 billion (estimates differ) during the early 1980s to make the Japanese firms in this industry competitive. All that money was spent for naught. None of the Japanese firms appreciably improved their market shares, and the two world leaders in the industry today are American (Intel) and South Korean (Samsung). Singapore spent about $15 billion in 1995 as part of a similar drive, as did China in 1999. Both policies were failures—no companies from either nation have managed to crack the top ten.

Britain tried similar maneuvers, just as it tried to prop up some of its ailing car companies. Both efforts failed. France spent billions trying to construct an information technology industry, a move that ultimately failed also. The simple fact is that the more globally competitive an industry is, the harder it is for government industrial policy to effectively promote companies in that industry. And because virtually all major industries are globally competitive, this means that industrial policy is destined to fail.

PICKING WINNERS—NOT AS EASY AS IT SEEMS

Most industrial policy is based on the belief of government officials that they are able to pick winners. Whether the selection process is undertaken in a poor country or in a rich country does not seem to matter, for reasons that are easy to understand. Consider the incentives facing government employees in charge of industrial policy compared to the incentives of decision makers in the private sector. First, the government policymaker is using other people's money—taxpayer dollars, yen, or euros. It is difficult for us to imagine that a government employee using other people's money is going to make better predictions about which industries or companies are going to be winners in the future than someone who has "skin in the game." After all, if the government employee is wrong, the financial consequences are minimal. Her or his life savings are not at stake.

There is also a certain amount of arrogance involved in a government official deciding where best to move resources in the economy. Under what circumstances would such an official have better information about future demands for certain products or services than people in the private sector? There are almost none of which we can think.[1] After all, those who pick winners in the private sector are rewarded handsomely and can become millionaires or even billionaires. In contrast, a government official who is successful in this endeavor might move up a grade level in civil service rating or perhaps be mentioned as an exemplary employee. Small peanuts, we would say.

CREATIVE DESTRUCTION AND BANKRUPTCY

Do you know what a Polaroid camera is? Probably not, because that good has virtually disappeared due to competition from a better instant photography medium—digital cameras. Do you know what an eight-track cassette tape is? Probably not. It was replaced by the compact disc, which is now becoming obsolete because of competition from online music downloading. Have you ever heard of FedMart? Probably not.

---

1 The (possible) exceptions involve industries (such as aerospace) where correct decision making is heavily dependent on "top secret," government-held information.

It was eventually put out of business by innovative competitors, such as WalMart.

A Harvard economist named Joseph Schumpeter (1883–1950) had a term for the death of certain companies over time—**creative destruction.** He used this term to describe the process by which the economy is transformed by innovation. In his view (now generally shared by economists), innovative entry by entrepreneurs is the economic force behind sustained long-term **economic growth.** In the process of innovation, the value of established companies (and many of their specialized workers) is destroyed. Of course, at the same time, even *more* value is created elsewhere by the innovation. Indeed, the process of creative destruction is at the heart of sustained economic growth.

We see most dramatically the process of innovative destruction at work when we see companies going **bankrupt.** Many companies simply disappear when they go bankrupt, forcing employees to seek work elsewhere. Other companies emerge from bankruptcy leaner and better able to compete. When a bankrupt company emerges from bankruptcy, most of its creditors and shareholders have lost considerable sums. Many of its workers have been laid off or have had to accept reduced salaries and benefits, even if they previously had a union contract. That is what would have happened, without taxpayer subsidies, for GM, Chrysler, Citicorp, Goldman Sachs, and AIG.

But What About Saving Jobs?

Whether bankruptcy is involved or not, creative destruction necessarily means that people will have to move from one job to another—old jobs are eliminated, new ones created. Supporters of the too-big-to-fail theory (and of industrial policy in general) always argue that they are only trying to "save jobs." It is true that such taxpayer subsidies may protect the jobs of those in the subsidized companies or industries. But that is hardly job-saving **fiscal policy.** Every subsidy to save a job in a company or industry has to be paid for. Either there is less government spending (and presumably fewer jobs) elsewhere or taxes must be raised, which means less taxpayer spending (and presumably fewer jobs) elsewhere. Therefore, a job "saved" in one company or industry ultimately leads to job *losses* in unsubsidized companies and industries. (In fact, there is every reason to believe that the jobs lost will *exceed* the jobs saved—see Chapter 25.) Economists are fond of saying that there is no such thing as a free lunch, and this principle applies to any fiscal policy justified as being purportedly "job saving."

Negative Industrial Policy

Despite all the talk by politicians about "saving" jobs, governments at all levels in the United States regularly have acted in ways that *reduce* employment. Indeed, the tax and regulatory policies of the federal government and many state governments have fostered a climate of **deindustrialization.** We have the second highest corporate tax rate in the world. Perhaps equally important, federal government regulations add dramatically to the cost of production in this country. Estimates of the annual costs go as high as $1.7 trillion for federal regulations, or about 12 percent of annual national income.

Businesses in the United States today are also facing regulatory uncertainty. They do not know whether there is going to be a tax on carbon output. They certainly do not know how to estimate the costs of the 2,400-page health care law or the 2,300-page financial services law, both passed in 2010. The latter requires that 243 new rules be written and no one knows what they will be. The former involves over a hundred new agencies, all of which will write new rules. All of this uncertainty puts U.S. companies at a disadvantage to their competitors in other countries, particularly in Asia.

The bottom line is simple. Despite their willingness to spend your money on bailouts, politicians don't actually seem too interested in promoting the policies that would encourage long-run recruiting and retention of workers. Once again, good politics makes bad economic policy.

For Critical Analysis

1. Who benefits and who loses from our "too-big-to-fail" policies?

2. Why do you think politicians are more active creating industrial policies during recessions than during boom times?

3. Estimated U.S. taxpayer subsidies in green energy technology through 2013 are about $125 billion. Under what circumstances does the federal government need to undertake these subsidies as opposed to letting private companies themselves pay for such investments?

4. Outline the scenario of what would have happened to GM had the federal government allowed it to go bankrupt on its own several years ago?

5. What is the incentive that private companies have to "pick winners"?

6. Is there any way to stop creative destruction?

CHAPTER 17

The Pension Crisis

It is never too early to think of your future. We refer not to your future classes or what you will do when you graduate. Nor do we speak of your future family, should you choose to have one. And not your self-imposed plan to stay healthy in the future. Rather, you might want to start thinking about how big your pension will be when you retire. That may seem a long way off, but for some—those who go to work for some cities and for some states—your pension might start in just 20 years.

CALIFORNIA ISN'T CALLED THE "GOLDEN" STATE FOR NOTHING

Today, in the face of one of its most serious fiscal crises ever, California taxpayers are footing the bill for former police officers, firefighters, and prison guards who can retire at age fifty with a pension that equals 90 percent of their final year's salary. There are more than fifteen thousand government retirees in California who receive pensions that exceed $100,000 per year (and this does not count payments from federal taxpayers through the Social Security system).

Consider the odd case of Gary Clift. He spent twenty-six years in the California Department of Corrections & Rehabilitation. Then he retired. He now collects 78 percent of the $112,000 salary he earned in his last year of work. He also gets full health care coverage for life, which adds a tidy sum to his retirement package. Ironically, Clift spent his last two years at work analyzing legislation that would raise the state's expenditures on retirement benefits. He got nowhere when he raised a red flag about increasing pension costs. As he said, "It's just taxpayers' money, so nobody cares."

Before we go any further with the relationship between government pension payments and California's fiscal problems, let's first look at the concept of retirement and pensions.

TO RETIRE, NORMALLY YOU HAVE TO SAVE

If we look back in time far enough, the concept of retirement did not exist. Individuals worked until they were physically unable to continue, and died soon thereafter. That was back when just about everyone in the world was poor. Those who could not work were often cared for by family members in large households. Not surprisingly, in very poor countries today, having lots of kids continues to be a form of retirement security—in fact, they may be the only thing standing between a retiree and starvation.

Through **economic growth,** individuals in many nations have been able to **save** in order to create **wealth** that can be used later on. If you do not **consume** everything that you earn, you can put aside funds to purchase houses and to make investments. Hence, when you choose to give up gainful employment, you have a stock of wealth that you can draw down during your remaining years.

If you work for a large company or a government, your retirement benefits will likely come from a pension plan run by your employer. Hopefully (for you), your employer will put aside funds in investments that will yield enough income to provide you with your promised pension. If the actual **rates of return** on these investments turn out to be as predicted by the pension plan, then there will be enough funding for all employees who retire to receive their promised pensions. If this condition is satisfied, we say that the employer (company or government) has a **fully funded pension liability.** Whenever employers do not set aside enough funds to cover future pensions, we say that they have **unfunded pension liabilities**. Now let's go back to the state of California to see how it has become the king of unfunded liabilities.

THE GOLDEN STATE TURNS RED

The term "red ink" usually refers to losses being suffered by a private company or to current year **budget deficits** incurred by a government entity. In recent years, California's red ink of this variety has been in the neighborhood of $10–$20 billion per year. But current California budget deficits are peanuts compared to its unfunded liabilities, mainly due to contractually guaranteed future pensions for its employees.

In the last dozen years, California state revenues—mainly from taxes—increased about 25 percent. Pension costs for that state's public employees, in contrast, increased by about 2,000 percent. No, that is not a typo. Recall our example of Gary Clift above. When he retired from the Department of Corrections & Rehabilitation, he was eligible to apply for a disability "bonus" that would have added many thousands of dollars to his pension every year. Gary had this option not because was disabled, but because the state of California says that working for the Department of Corrections is stressful—and so an employee *might* become disabled. Gary didn't put in for the disability bonus, but he was the only manager at the prison where he worked that did not.

California's problem is more widespread than simply the prisons, however. In the 1960s, about 5 percent of retiring California state workers received so-called public safety pensions. That meant the individuals had been working in a "dangerous" job. Today, about 35 percent of retiring state workers obtain this "public safety" retirement bonus, which was intended originally just for firefighters and police officers. In addition, California is the only state that uses the last year of an employee's salary to determine her or his long-term pension benefits, rather than averaging over the salaries of the last several years of work. Because pay usually rises over time, California's method generates extra pension benefits—and extra liabilities for taxpayers.

But there is more. Every year for decades, the legislature in Sacramento has improved public pension benefits. Consider just one of those improvements, passed in 1999. It was supposed to cost the state about $650 million per year by 2010. It actually cost $3.1 billion in 2010 and $3.5 billion in 2011.

Okay, so how bad can it be—a few billion here and a few billion there? Well, some studies have estimated that California has a $500 billion unfunded pension liability problem. And this problem cannot go away by itself because the courts have consistently upheld government employee pension benefits as untouchable contracts, except in a few rare cases in which a local government declares bankruptcy. In one recent year alone, over $3 billion of California state spending was diverted to pension costs from other programs. The diversion of state spending to fund pensions seems certain to do nothing but rise in the future.

A Closer Look at the "Garden State"

New Jersey, the self-described "garden state," is starting to look wilted. It, too, has been running billions of dollars of pension red ink per year. By the latest estimates, the New Jersey employee pension fund is well over $30 billion in the hole. What does that mean for a typical four-member household in New Jersey? Each is on the hook for about $16,000 in tax liabilities, just to make up this underfunding.

How did New Jersey get in this mess? Well, as in California, a big part of the problem started back in the 1990s. The stock market was booming, producing high rates of return on state investments. Under the assumption that these abnormally high returns were the new reality, state legislatures enhanced retirement benefits. Two stock market crashes later, the hoped-for returns haven't materialized, but the promised pensions are still there.

THE TOTAL PICTURE

Throughout the United States, only four states—Florida, New York, Washington, and Wisconsin—have well-funded pension systems. The remaining states are facing different degrees of fiscal disaster. Illinois and Kansas, for example, have enough assets on hand to pay for only 50–60 percent of their pension liabilities.

The PEW Center on the States did an exhaustive study just prior to the 2008 financial meltdown, and concluded that the fifty states had a $1 *trillion* pension funding gap. The states combined had contractually promised $3.35 trillion in pension, health, and other retirement benefits but only had $2.35 trillion on hand to pay for them. In all likelihood this $1 trillion gap is much greater today because of stock market losses since 2008, and the fact that most states still have unrealistic assumptions about future rates of return. (And, by the way, cities are also in deep trouble. One conservative estimate puts the funding gap for them at nearly $600 billion.)

THE PRIVATE SECTOR HAS PROBLEMS, TOO

Don't think that government decision makers at the state and local level have been the only ones to create unfunded pension liabilities. In the private sector, large corporations have found themselves with growing pension funding problems. One major company that has long loved to hide future pension liabilities is General Motors. In an effort to report better earnings, that company routinely used aggressive accounting practices and made pension contributions that were just a fraction of what it really needed to make. Eventually, though, GM's actual pension promises became due. When the company tried to pay for these costs by hiking the price of the cars it manufactured, those cars quickly became uncompetitive. Consumers started buying other brands that were cheaper for the same quality. The result was GM bankruptcy and a federal takeover. Taxpayers own a high percentage of shares in "Government Motors," as it is now sometimes called. Hence, taxpayers are now on the hook for future pension liabilities of the company.

GM is not alone. Over 75 percent of the largest five hundred corporations in the United States have unfunded pension fund obligations. It is perhaps no surprise that many of these companies have lobbied Congress to let them off the hook from meeting their legal obligations to more fully fund their pension plans.

BANKRUPTCIES ON THE HORIZON?

Returning our examination to the public sector, even though you may not be expecting to retire for decades, your economic well-being is already changing because of retirement commitments that cities and states have already made. In order to fulfill those unfunded pension liabilities, city and state governments are cutting back on essential services—education, police and prisons, and firefighters. You might think that we should not or "cannot" let essential government services be cut back just to pay pension benefits. Right now that is reality, however, all across the country.

Is there a way to reduce unfunded pension liabilities? Yes, but it is ugly. Just ask the residents of Vallejo, California. In 2008, eighteen police personnel and firefighters unexpectedly retired early. That city of 120,000 was immediately obligated to pay out several million dollars for their first year of retirement. This is a city that was already forking over $220 million for pensions and health care. Vallejo City government filed for **bankruptcy.**

Under so-called Chapter 9 of our **Bankruptcy Code,** municipal governments can propose their own reorganization plans and void union contracts without having to sell off their assets, such as buildings and investments. The public pension obligations of Vallejo were lumped together with all the rest of its obligations. Everyone from private accounting firms to public pensioners who were owed money had to take a "haircut"— accept less than 100 cents on the dollar owed. So now we see at least one way that cities, indeed, even states, can get out of the jam in which they find themselves. Declaring bankruptcy can allow them to renegotiate future pension benefits to put them more in line with future funding possibilities.

Right now, some cities are defaulting on the loans that they took out in past years. In a recent year, $3 billion in city debt was not paid when it came due. As we have already seen, that is a trivial amount compared to total unfunded pension liabilities. When more municipal governments choose to go bankrupt, the rate of municipal bond defaults will increase accordingly. This process will be painful and costly for retirees and bondholders alike. But the simple fact is this: State and local governments have been making promises they cannot realistically keep. Something must give and that means one of three things must happen. State and local spending on other programs must be slashed, taxes have to be hiked dramatically, or pensions need to be cut. Eventually, the easy political promises of the past must collide with the hard economic reality of the future.

WHY ISN'T THE FEDERAL GOVERNMENT IN THE SAME FIX?

As you might have noticed, there has been little discussion of the federal government's retirement system to which all of us contribute—**Social Security.** The reason is that Social Security is a **pay-as-you-go system.** The federal government has *not* taken your Social Security "contributions" and invested them in some special account. Indeed, there is no "account" earning interest now so that it will be there with your name on it when you choose to retire in your sixties. While you may have heard about something called a Social Security trust fund, that fund is just on paper. It's a myth, and a huge liability itself, about which you will learn more in Chapter 19.

FOR CRITICAL ANALYSIS

1. If there is no government- or company-provided pension system, how can an individual create a financially safe retirement?

2. Why would a state or local government ever commit more resources for future pension benefits than it could possibly have resources to pay?

3. Many state and local governments have been using an assumed 8 percent rate of return figure when calculating future funding of promised pension benefits. Why do you suppose they used this rather than an assumption of 2 percent, or even 0 percent?

4. Why can't state and local governments simply continue to borrow funds through the bond market to cover not only shortfalls in current tax revenues but also shortfalls in future available funding to pay contractual pension benefits?

5. The grim economic climate since 2008 has caused many workers to defer their retirements. How will this affect large employers in state and local governments?

6. In the private sector, one in five workers have been promised lifetime pensions. In the public sector, four in five workers have lifetime pensions. Why does the private sector offer so few lifetime pensions compared to the public sector?

CHAPTER 18

Higher Taxes Are in Your Future

"These road improvements of $241,000,000 were paid for:

86 percent from the Federal Highway Trust Fund
12 percent from state funds
2 percent from local funds."

Most of you have seen at least one sign similar to this while driving somewhere in the United States. If you have ever driven anywhere in Europe, you see comparable signs, but they usually have a longer list of "contributors." The parallel, though, is that the "contributors" are government agencies, not *you*. Now, it would be nice to think that funds for highway improvement projects come from the moon or Mars or even from the bank account of some foreign oil mogul. But they do not.

THOSE PESKY BUDGET CONSTRAINTS

Government does not exist independently of those who live, work, spend, and pay taxes in our society. As an economy, we face a **budget constraint.** Whatever is spent by government—federal, state, or local—is not and cannot be spent by individuals in the nation. Whatever government commands in terms of spending decisions, private individuals do not command. All of those dollars available for spending on final goods and services in the United States can be controlled by you, the private citizen, or government. Otherwise stated, what the government spends, you don't spend. It is as simple as that, despite the periodic efforts of government (especially at the national level) to conceal the truth of this budget constraint.

STIMULUS AND BAILOUT

Early in 2008, as the recession of 2007–2009 worsened, President Bush proposed, and Congress enacted, an "economic stimulus" package said to cost $152 billion. Most of the package consisted of tax cuts that were supposed to raise disposable income, and thus produce an increase in private spending.

Later in the year, as the recession continued to worsen and financial panic hit, the President and Congress reacted by bailing out some of the biggest financial companies in America, including insurance giant AIG. Although the total cost of the bill still has not been determined, the legislation called for up to $700 billion in taxpayer funds to be used to prop up these companies.

Just a few months later, newly elected President Obama successfully pushed Congress to pass yet another stimulus package, this one said to cost $787 billion. This legislation provided additional money for extended unemployment benefits, and also transferred hundreds of billions of dollars to state and local governments.

Not long afterwards (ironically, just as the recession was officially ending) President Obama pushed for and got funds to bail out the major American automobile companies. Ford declined the funds, but both General Motors and Chrysler accepted the money, enough in the case of GM to make taxpayers of the United States majority shareholders in the company.

Taken together, the stimulus and bailout programs enacted over this eighteen-month period had a price tag of somewhere between $1.5 and $2 trillion. Much of these funds were borrowed, thereby generating the largest federal budget deficits in American history. And because all of these new debts will have to be repaid, higher taxes are in your future.

INCREASED SPENDING, INCREASED TAXES

When Congress passes legislation to spend more, whether it is for bailing out the financial sector, improving education and public infrastructure, or attempting to reduce poverty, there is ultimately only one place it can obtain the resources. That place is you and everyone else who earns income each year in the United States. As we noted in Chapters 13 and 14, having the ability to run a larger federal government deficit (and thus increase the net national debt) does not change the fundamental budget constraint facing our society.

What government spends, the rest of us do not spend. Perhaps without your realizing it, your **real tax rate** has already gone up in the last several years. Why? Because federal government spending has increased as a share of **gross domestic product (GDP).** Your real tax rate is easily calculated. It is the percentage of GDP controlled by the government. The observed taxes that you pay through automatic withholding of federal income taxes on your wages or salary will eventually catch up. The budget constraint guarantees that.

But What About All Those Tax Cuts?

By the time the election of 2010 rolled around, taxpayers were finally starting to get nervous about all of this new federal spending. This was surely one of the reasons that so many Democrats were voted out of office in that election. The first thing Congress did after the election was to extend tax cuts passed back in 2001 and 2003, during the Bush Administration. Moreover, Congress extended unemployment benefits (even though the recession had ended eighteen months before) and even enacted a temporary cut in the payroll taxes used to finance Social Security.

As we discussed more fully in Chapter 13, we really cannot expect these tax cuts to increase aggregate demand. Because government spending was not reduced, the burden of the government was not reduced. The net effect was to raise the deficit relative to what it would have been, and make the necessary eventual tax increases even larger. No matter what the politicians promise, the budget constraint cannot be avoided. Hence, higher taxes are in your future. But because **marginal tax rates** were reduced as part of this package, we can expect people to work more, produce more, and thus earn more because they get to keep more of what they earn. This so-called "supply side" effect of the lower tax rates will indeed help the economy recover faster from the recession of 2007–2009.

Who Gets the Bill?

Although almost 220 million personal tax returns are filed with the Internal Revenue Service every year, many of these filers pay no federal income taxes at all. In fact, about 47 percent of "taxpayers" either pay no federal income taxes or actually pay *negative* federal income taxes because they receive **tax credits.** Under a tax credit, people who pay no federal income taxes effectively get a check from the federal government, which they can use to pay other federal taxes they might owe (such as Social Security) or to pay *future* federal tax liabilities, should they arise. And if there are no current or likely future tax liabilities, well, they get to keep the cash.

There may well be perfectly good reasons to effectively exempt some people from paying income taxes, perhaps because they are impoverished, or have major medical bills. But it is important to recognize two implications of shielding large numbers of people from income taxes. First, this helps create the impression for many voters that federal spending is effectively "free"—because, after all, they will not be responsible when the bills come due. Thus, they are more likely to favor expansion of government spending that does not confer benefits that exceed its costs. This reduces the overall wealth of society. Second, with large numbers of individuals exempt from federal income taxes, the burden on those who *do* pay taxes is that much greater. This will induce such people to work less, produce less, and earn less because they get to keep less of what they earn. And this lower production means that the wealth of society is reduced.

Is Argentina Showing the Way?

Argentina was one of the ten richest countries in the world a hundred years ago. It has since slipped to about seventieth on that list. Over the same period of time, government spending (and taxes) in Argentina has been growing relative to the overall size of the economy. Most recently, Argentine president Cristina Kirchner announced that the nation's private pension system was being taken over by the national government. While she claimed that it was for the "good of the people" because the market was too risky for retirement savings, in fact President Kirchner wanted to use those assets to fund more government spending. Technically, the government will "borrow" from the retirement system. But because the Argentine government has a track record of defaulting on its borrowings, many people expect that they will get back few, if any, of their hard-earned retirement pesos.

As you might expect, contributions into the private pension plan plummeted as soon as the government announced its plan. Some Argentine citizens quietly began moving other **assets** out of the country, hoping to protect them from similar confiscation. Still others began making plans for moving *themselves* out of the country, on the grounds that emigration was the ultimate form of protection.

The Argentine government's nationalization of the private pension system is simply a once-and-for-all increase in taxes. While it is unlikely that the U.S. government would seek to take control of private pension plans here, the Argentine story illustrates the key point of this chapter. What the government spends, we must pay for. Sometimes the government must be creative in making that happen, but happen it will. Hence our prediction: Higher taxes are in your future.

FOR CRITICAL ANALYSIS

1. The government now owns shares of stock and warrants in many banks, insurance companies, some auto companies, and other sectors of the economy. (Warrants are rights to own future shares of stock.) If the value of the shares owned by the federal government increases because the market price per share rises, in what way could this increase actually permit a reduction in future taxes? Explain.

2. If you are a lower-income-earning individual and thus pay no income taxes, should you care about tax increases for other individuals? Explain.

3. Is it *possible* that in, say, ten years, the real tax rate paid by U.S. residents will be lower than it is today? What circumstances would have to change to make this occur? Explain.

4. Who, exactly, will be paying the higher future taxes implied by the stimulus packages, tax cuts, and bailouts of 2008–2010? (*Hint:* Look in the mirror.)

5. Why do most politicians love to spend money and hate to pay for their expenditures? Is this attitude different from the one you have toward making purchases as opposed to paying for those purchases? What are the consequences for you if you spend more than your income?

6. Most states have laws or constitutional provisions that require them to quickly eliminate any budget deficits by either raising taxes or cutting spending. Can you suggest why states would have this rule but the federal government would not?

CHAPTER 19

The Myths of Social Security

You have probably heard politicians debate the need to reform Social Security. If you are under the age of 30, this debate has been going on for your entire lifetime. Why has nothing been done? The reason is that the politicians are debating over "facts" that are not facts: Most of the claims made about Social Security are myths—urban legends, if you like. Sadly, the politicians have been repeating these myths so often for so long that they believe them, and so do their constituents (perhaps including you). As long as these myths persist, nothing meaningful will be done about Social Security, and the problem will simply get worse. So let's see if we can't cut through the fog by examining some of the worst Social Security myths.

MYTH 1: THE ELDERLY ARE POOR

The Social Security Act was passed in 1935 as the United States was emerging from the Great Depression. The **unemployment rate** at the time was the highest in our nation's history. **Bank runs** and the stock market crash of 1929 had wiped out the savings of millions of people. Many elderly people had few or no **resources** to draw on in retirement, and their extended families often had few resources with which to help them. In the midst of these conditions, Social Security was established to make sure that the elderly had access to some *minimum* level of income when they retired. It was never meant to be the sole source of retirement funds for senior citizens.

Given the circumstances of the program's founding, it is not surprising that many people associate Social Security with poverty among the elderly. The fact is that both the Social Security program and the financial condition of older people have changed dramatically over the years. For example, measured in inflation-adjusted dollars, initial Social Security payments were as little as $120 per month and reached a maximum of $500 per month, or about $6,000 per year. Today, however, many recipients are eligible for payments well in excess of $25,000 per year. More important, people over age 65 are no longer among the poorest in our society.

Despite the ravages of the recession of 2007–2009, today's elderly have accumulated literally *trillions* of dollars in **assets.** These assets include homes and substantial portfolios of stocks and **bonds.** In addition, millions of older Americans are drawing *private* pensions, built up over years of employment. Social Security payments, for example, now provide only about 40 percent of the income of the average retired person, with the rest coming about equally from private pensions, employment earnings, and investment income. Far from being the age group with the highest poverty rate, the elderly actually suffer about 25 percent *less* poverty than the average of all U.S. residents. To be sure, Social Security helps make this possible, but just as surely, only about 10 percent of the elderly are living in poverty. In contrast, the poverty rate among children is twice as high as it is among people over age 65.

Myth 2: Social Security Is Fixed Income

Most economic and political commentators and laypersons alike treat Social Security benefits as a source of fixed income for the elderly, one that supposedly falls in **real purchasing power** as the general **price level** rises. This myth, too, has its roots in the early days of Social Security, when payments were indeed fixed in dollar terms and thus were potentially subject to the ravages of **inflation.** But this is no longer true. In 1972, Congress decided to link Social Security payments to a measure of the overall price level in the economy. The avowed reason for this change was to protect Social Security payments from any decline in real value during inflation. In fact, because of the price level measure chosen by Congress, the real value of payments actually rises when there is inflation.

Although there are many potential measures of the average price of goods and services, Congress decided to tie Social Security payments to the **consumer price index (CPI).** The CPI is supposed to measure changes in the dollar cost of consuming a bundle of goods and services that is representative for the typical consumer. Thus, a 10 percent rise in the CPI is supposed to mean that the **cost of living** has gone up by 10 percent. Accordingly, the law provides that Social Security benefits are automatically increased by 10 percent.

As it turns out, however, the CPI actually overstates the true inflation rate: It is *biased upward* as a measure of inflation. This bias has several sources. For example, when the price of a good rises relative to other prices, people usually consume less of it, enabling them to avoid some of the added cost of the good. But the CPI does not take this into account. Similarly, although the average quality of goods and services generally rises over time, the CPI does not adequately account for this fact. Overall, it has been estimated that until recently, the upward bias in the CPI amounted to about 1.1 percentage points per year on average. Revisions to the CPI have reduced this bias to about 0.8 percent per year. Thus currently, if the CPI says prices have gone up, say, 1.8 percent, they've really gone up only 1.0 percent. Nevertheless, Social Security payments are automatically increased by the full 1.8 percent.

Now, 0.8 or 1.1 percentage points don't sound like much. And if it happened only once or twice, there wouldn't be much of a problem. But almost every year for forty years, this extra amount has been added to benefits. And over a long time, even the small upward bias begins to amount to a real change in **purchasing power.** Indeed, this provision of the Social Security system has had the cumulative effect of raising real (inflation-adjusted) Social Security benefits by about 50 percent over this period. So despite the myth that Social Security is fixed income, in reality the benefits grow even faster than inflation.

Myth 3: There Is a Social Security Trust Fund

For the first few years of Social Security's existence, taxes were collected but no benefits were paid. The funds collected were used to purchase U.S. Treasury bonds, and that accumulation of bonds was called the Social Security Trust Fund. Even today, tax collections (called **payroll taxes**) exceed benefits paid each year—currently by more than $150 billion per year—so that the trust fund now has well over $2 *trillion* in Treasury bonds on its books. Eventually, after the fund reaches a peak of around $2.6 trillion, retiring baby boomers will drive outgoing benefits above incoming tax collections. The bonds will be sold to finance the difference. By around 2040, all of them will be sold, and thereafter all benefits in excess of payroll taxes will have to be financed explicitly out of current taxes.

The standard story told (by politicians at least) is that the bonds in the trust fund represent net assets, much like the assets owned by private pension plans. *This is false.* Congress has already spent the past excess of taxes over benefits and has simply given the trust fund IOUs. These IOUs are called U.S. Treasury bonds, and they are nothing more than promises by the U.S. Treasury to levy taxes on someone to pay benefits. When it is time for the trust fund to redeem the IOUs it holds, Congress will have to raise taxes, cut spending on other programs, or borrow more to raise the funds. But this would be true even if there were *no* Treasury bonds in the trust fund: All Social Security benefits must ultimately be paid for out of taxes. So whatever might have been intended for the trust fund, the only asset actually backing that fund is nothing more and nothing less than an obligation of Americans—you—to pay taxes in the future.

MYTH 4: SOCIAL SECURITY WILL BE THERE FOR YOU

Social Security was a great deal for Ida Mae Fuller, who in 1940 became the first person to receive a regular Social Security pension. She had paid a total of $25 in Social Security taxes before she retired. By the time she died in 1975 at the age of 100, she had received benefits totaling $23,000. And although Ida Mae did better than most recipients, the *average* annual real rate of return for those early retirees was an astounding 135 percent *per year.* (That is, after adjusting for inflation, every initial $100 in taxes paid yielded $135 *per year* during each and every year of that person's retirement.)

People retiring more recently have not done quite so well, but everyone who retired by about 1970 has received a far better return from Social Security than could likely have been obtained from any other investment. These higher benefits relative to contributions were made possible because at each point in time, *current retirees are paid benefits out of the taxes paid by individuals who are currently working.* Social Security is a **pay-as-you-go system.** It is not like a true retirement plan in which participants pay into a fund and receive benefits according to what they have paid in and how much that fund has cumulatively earned. So as long as Social Security was pulling in enough new people each year, the system could offer benefits that were high relative to taxes paid. But the number of people paying Social Security taxes is no longer growing so fast, and the number of retirees is growing faster. Moreover, today's trickle of new retirees is becoming tomorrow's flood as the baby boom generation exits the workforce. The result is bad news all around.

One way to think about the problem facing us—which is chiefly a problem facing *you*—is to contemplate the number of retirees each worker must support. In 1945, forty-two workers shared the burden of each Social Security recipient. By 1960, nine workers had to pick up the tab for each person collecting Social Security. Today, the burden of a retiree is spread out among slightly more than four workers. By 2030 or so, fewer than three workers will be available to pay the Social Security benefits due each recipient.

The coming tax bill for all of this will be staggering. If we *immediately* raised Social Security (payroll) taxes from 15.3 percent to a bit over 19 percent—more than a 24 percent increase—and kept them there for the next seventy-five years or so, the system's revenues would probably be large enough to meet its obligations. But this would be the largest tax increase in U.S. history, which makes it extremely unlikely that it will occur. Yet every day that Congress delays, the situation gets worse. If Congress waits until 2030 to raise taxes, they will have to be increased by more than 50 percent. Indeed, some commentators are predicting that without fundamental reforms to the system, payroll taxes *alone* will have to be hiked to 25 percent of wages—in addition to regular federal, state, and local income taxes, of course.

And what are any reforms likely to be? Well, rules will specify that people must be older before they become eligible for Social Security benefits. Existing legislation has already scheduled a hike in the age for full benefits up to 67 from its current 66. Almost certainly, this age threshold will be raised again, perhaps to seventy. Moreover, it is likely that all Social Security benefits (rather than just a portion) will eventually be subject to federal income taxes. It is even possible that some high-income individuals—you, perhaps—will be declared ineligible for benefits because their income from other sources is too high.

So what does all this mean for you? Well, technically, a Social Security system will probably be in existence when you retire, although the retirement age will be higher than today and benefits will have been scaled back significantly. It is also likely that, strictly speaking, the Social Security Trust Fund will still be around when you hit the minimum age for benefits. But whatever else happens to the Social Security system between now and your retirement, you can be secure in your knowledge of one thing: You will be getting a much bigger tax bill from the federal government to pay for it.

FOR CRITICAL ANALYSIS

1. Where has all of the Social Security money gone?

2. People over the age of 65 have been highly successful in protecting and enhancing the real benefits they receive from Social Security. This has come at the expense of other people in society, particularly young people. What do you think explains the ability of older people to win political battles with younger people?

3. Analyze how each of the following hypothetical policy changes would affect people's decision to retire. Would the change induce people to retire sooner or later? Explain your reasoning.

   (a) An increase in the age at which one can receive full Social Security benefits (currently age 66 to 67, depending on the year in which a person was born)
   (b) A decrease in the fraction (currently 75 percent) of full benefits that one can receive if retirement occurs at age 62
   (c) An increase in the Medicare eligibility age from its current level of 65
   (d) An increase to 100 percent from its current 85 percent in the maximum fraction of Social Security benefits that is subject to the federal income tax

4. If a person starts collecting Social Security benefits before full retirement age but also continues to work, then for each $2 in income earned (above a modest level), that person's benefits are reduced by $1. What is the effective **marginal tax rate** imposed by the Social Security system on such earnings from work? Explain.

5. For each year after full retirement age that a person delays collecting Social Security benefits, the annual benefits are raised by 8 percent. (This "bump" in benefits ceases at age 70. Additional retirement delays do not cause benefits to rise any further.) How is the incentive to retire prior to age 70 affected by this provision for benefit increments, relative to a system in which benefits were not raised in this manner? Explain.

6. What does the existence of the Social Security system do to the incentive of a worker to save for his or her retirement? What does it do to the worker's incentive to save to provide an inheritance for his or her children? Explain.

PART FOUR

Monetary Policy and Financial Institutions

CHAPTER 20

The Fed and Financial Panics

The Panic of 1907 began after a failed attempt by Otto Heinze to "corner the market" on **shares of stock** in the United Copper Company. Heinze had expected the demand for United's shares to increase in the near term and thought that if he bought up enough shares quickly at low prices, he could turn around and sell them at a handsome **profit.** His judgment proved wrong, and Heinze had to sell out at devastatingly low prices. Not only did his stock brokerage firm go out of business as a result. More disastrously, the public's confidence in the financial condition of banks that had large holdings of United Copper shares evaporated. Confidence also plummeted regarding the financial health of several banks with whom Otto's brother Augustus was associated.

All of these banks suffered **bank runs,** in which large numbers of customers simultaneously withdrew their deposits, and some ultimately failed as a result. The banking panic soon spread more widely, threatening the security of the entire financial system. It was eventually halted only when the famed financier J.P. Morgan induced a large number of banks to join a consortium and mutually stand behind each other's financial obligations.

BIRTH OF THE FED

The Panic of 1907 achieved notoriety at the time by causing the recession of 1907–1908, but the panic's longer-term importance lies elsewhere. Hoping to avoid a repeat of 1907's financial meltdown, Congress in 1913 established the **Federal Reserve System,** commonly referred to as the **Fed.** The Fed is now the nation's monetary authority and, among other things, our first line of defense against financial panics.

As had been true in prior financial panics, the crux of many banks' woes in 1907 was their inability to convert their assets into the cash that panicked depositors desperately wanted. So the Fed was created to serve as "lender of last resort" to the nation's **commercial banks.** Congress empowered the Fed to lend funds to banks to meet whatever demands that depositors put on the banks, regardless of how great those demands might be. The intention was that there would never be another financial panic in the United States, an objective that, if achieved, would significantly reduce the number and severity of the nation's economic **recessions.**

OPPORTUNITY AND FAILURE

The Fed's first real chance to perform as lender of last resort—the function for which it was created—came in 1930 when several prominent New York banks got into financial difficulties. Customers of those and other banks started withdrawing funds, fearing that their banks might be weak. This spreading lack of confidence was exactly the scenario the Fed was created to defend against—yet it did nothing. The result was a banking panic and a worsening of the economic downturn already under way.

The next year, the Fed had two more opportunities to act as lender of last resort when confidence in banks sagged, yet in both cases it again failed to act. The results were recurring bank panics in 1931 and an intensification of what was by then an extremely severe recession. Early in 1933, eroding public confidence in the banking system gave the Fed yet another opportunity to step in as lender of last resort, and *again* it failed to do so. The resulting banking panic was disastrous and ushered in the deepest stages of what has come to be known as the Great Depression. It is little wonder that Herbert Hoover, who was president of the United States at the time, referred to the Fed as "a weak reed for a nation to lean on in time of trouble."

LESSONS LEARNED

Thirty years after the end of the Great Depression, Nobel laureate Milton Friedman and Anna Schwartz published *A Monetary History of the United States.* Among other things, this book laid out in detail the story of the Fed's failings during the 1930s. The book's lessons were absorbed by at least two people who have since served as the head of the Fed— Alan Greenspan, who was chair of the Fed from 1987 to 2006, and Ben Bernanke, who succeeded Greenspan.

Greenspan's opportunity to have the Fed serve as the banking system's lender of last resort came in September 2001, in the wake of the terrorist attacks on the World Trade Center towers. Banks found themselves in need of a quick infusion of funds as panicked depositors made large-scale withdrawals of cash. The Fed quickly stepped in to provide funds to banks, enabling them to meet the demands of depositors without having to sell off **assets** quickly at depressed prices. A terrorist attack had surely never been contemplated by the legislators who created the Fed. Nevertheless, the Fed acted vigorously as a lender of last resort and thus certainly achieved the objectives of its creators—prevention of financial panic.

THE PANIC OF '08

Only 2 years after he replaced Greenspan as chair of the Fed, Ben Bernanke had an even bigger opportunity to put the Fed to work. Late in 2008, rapidly eroding confidence in America's financial system led to the near or total collapse of several major financial firms. Many commercial banks, investment banks, and even insurance companies were suddenly in dire condition. Potential borrowers across the country found themselves unable to obtain funds from anyone, at any rate of interest. Although circumstances differed from 1907 in that commercial banks were not at the center of the panic, there was no doubt about one point: The Panic of '08 was just as threatening to the U.S. economy as its century-old predecessor had been.

Mindful of the costs of inaction, the Fed moved swiftly to maintain and restore confidence in key components of the financial system. But its actions were considerably broader than ever before. Historically, for example, the Fed has lent funds to commercial banks and to the federal government itself. But in 2008, the Fed also lent hundreds of billions of dollars directly to nonbank corporations around the country, including tens of billions to insurance giant AIG. The Fed also began purchasing obligations of government-sponsored **mortgage** market giants Fannie Mae and Freddie Mac, hoping to encourage more lending for home purchases. And finally, the Fed agreed to the following trade with commercial banks: It would exchange billions of dollars of risk-free federal **bonds** it held for billions of dollars of high-risk private bonds that they held. In effect, the Fed helped the banks remove high-risk assets of questionable value from their **balance sheets,** thus reducing the chances that skittish depositors might suddenly make large-scale withdrawals of funds from commercial banks.

THE SURGE IN EXCESS RESERVES

On many of their deposits, commercial banks are required to keep a minimum amount of **reserves** on hand, either in their vaults or on deposit with the Fed. These are referred to as **required reserves.** Any reserves above these minimum required levels are called **excess reserves.** Over the past 70 years, bank holdings of excess reserves have generally been quite small, amounting to no more than a few billion dollars for the entire banking system. And this is not surprising. In normal times, banks generally keep only enough excess reserves to handle day-to-day transactions with depositors because they can earn interest on any funds they lend out.

By 2009, excess reserves soared to more than $800 billion, and eventually topped $1.2 *trillion.* Total reserves (required plus excess) were up sharply because the Fed was giving banks reserves in return for other assets. Among the purchases were commercial paper (debts issued by private companies), securities backed by credit card debt and home mortgages, and even home mortgages themselves. But almost all of the Fed-provided reserves simply sat there—either in bank vaults or on deposit with the Fed—because banks lent almost none of them out.

Banks across the country held on to the excess reserves for three reasons. First, the sagging economy meant that borrowers were riskier and hence less profitable at any given interest rate. Second, depositors were greatly concerned about the financial condition of commercial banks. The banks therefore wanted plenty of funds on hand—in the form of excess reserves—in case they had to meet increased withdrawal demands by depositors. Oddly enough, the third reason for the failure of banks to lend out reserves was a new policy implemented by the Fed itself.

PAYING INTEREST ON RESERVES

In 2008, the Fed began paying interest on the reserves held by commercial banks, something it had never done before. And it was paying interest not just on required reserves but on *excess* reserves as well. This policy encouraged banks to hold excess reserves rather than to lend the funds to customers. Thus, the payment of interest on commercial bank reserves made it *more difficult* for companies and individuals to get loans. (See Chapter 21 for more on this.)

On balance, it remains to be seen whether the Fed actions during the last recession lived up to the expectations that the Fed's founders had more than a century ago. By providing funds to banks and other financial institutions, the Fed helped reduce the impact of the financial panic and helped prevent widespread runs on commercial banks. Nevertheless, the Fed decision to pay interest on reserves markedly discouraged banks from lending those reserves to companies and households across the land. This surely *slowed* recovery from the recession. Only time and further study will tell whether, on balance, the Fed's actions during the recession made us better off—or worse off.

For Critical Analysis

1. How did the Fed's long-standing policy of not paying interest on bank reserves act much like a tax on bank reserves?

2. If the Fed continued to pay interest on required reserves but stopped paying interest on excess reserves, how would bank lending incentives be changed?

3. If the Fed had not injected reserves into the banking system in 2008, what would have been the consequences for the banks and for **aggregate demand**?

4. By late 2010 concerns over bank solvency had faded. How did this change likely alter the incentives of banks to lend out excess reserves? What are the implications for aggregate demand? Explain.

5. In the long run, if the Fed fails to remove the excess reserves from the banking system, what will the banks do with them? What are the implications for inflation? Explain.

6. The Fed was given great power in 1913 to undertake potentially beneficial actions. Did this also give it great power to engage in potentially *harmful* actions? Explain why or why not.

CHAPTER 21

The Fed Feeding Frenzy

"QE1 didn't seem to work. But QE2 looks hopeful. When will QE3 have to be undertaken?"

If you have no idea what the above quote means, you are not alone. Here is the origin of the abbreviation "QE." Financial reporters decided a few years ago to accept a new term for an old concept. That term is **quantitative easing (QE).** Consequently, "QE1" is a reference to the Fed's expansionary monetary policy during the latest serious recession, in 2008 and 2009. QE2 refers to the Fed's expansionary monetary policy that started in November 2010. QE3—who knows?

MONETARY POLICY—THE WAY IT USED TO BE

Historically, the Fed's main tool for monetary policy has been the purchase and sale of U.S. government securities, usually **Treasury bills.** When the Fed has wanted to engage in expansionary monetary policy, it bought U.S. Treasuries in the **open market,** thereby increasing **reserves** in the banking system. **Excess reserves** (those over and above legally **required reserves**) were used by banks to expand loans. In the process, the **money supply** grew, which increased aggregate demand. Contractionary monetary policy was just the opposite—the Fed sold U.S. government securities, thereby reducing reserves. The end result was a decrease in the money supply in circulation and a decrease in aggregate demand.

That was then, but Fed monetary policy changed quite abruptly in response to the financial panic in late 2008.

THE FED STARTED TO LIKE OTHER ASSETS

During the first 95 years of its existence, the Federal Reserve dealt with U.S. government securities only. All that changed in 2008 when the Fed decided that it had to target specific sectors in our economy. So, instead of engaging in traditional expansionary monetary policy, the Fed started buying assets other than U.S. government securities. This was something that had never been done before.

The assets purchased by the Fed included (and still include) short-term corporate debt, short-term loans to banks, **mortgage-backed securities,** mostly issued by the government-sponsored corporations Fannie Mae and Freddie Mac, other debt issued by Fannie Mae and Freddie Mac, and preferred shares in the former investment bank Bear Stearns and in the insurance company American International Group (AIG). Oh, and let's not forget that for well over a year the Fed engaged in **foreign currency swaps** with other countries—perhaps that was considered the icing on the larger cake.

All of those purchases of all of those assets clearly increased the size and composition of the Fed's **balance sheet.** For much of its more recent existence, the Fed "owned" anywhere from several billion to several hundred billion dollars of U.S. Treasury securities. But by 2011, the Fed's assets totaled close to $2.5 trillion (including many hundreds of billions in "new" securities it had bought as part of its quantitative easing policy).

So, in a sentence, the Fed's traditional monetary policy abruptly changed in 2008. Rather than seeking to stimulate the entire economy in general, the Fed decided to provide credit to parts of financial markets (and even specific corporations) that it believed were being abandoned by private lenders. Never before in its history had the chair of the Fed and its board of directors used such discretionary policy to benefit specific sectors of the economy.

WHY WASN'T THERE AN OUTBREAK OF INFLATION?

With traditional monetary policy analysis, when the Fed aggressively adds to the money supply in circulation by buying U.S. government securities, the banking system suddenly has excess reserves. Not wanting to lose out on potential income from those excess reserves, depository institutions increase their loans, the money supply rises, and aggregate demand increases. At least that's the way economists used to tell the story.

While QE1, QE2, and so forth, got the headlines, however, there was a revolution in central banking in the United States. Starting on October 1, 2008, the Fed began paying interest on reserves—*all* reserves, including excess reserves. While some monetary economists for years have argued that interest should be paid on required reserves, none ever demanded that interest be paid on excess reserves, too. This policy change by the Fed converted excess reserves into an income-earning asset for banks, and thus fundamentally altered the nature of the conduct of monetary policy.

If you are the manager of a bank and know that the Fed will pay interest on excess reserves, you are not so keen to loan out those reserves to businesses and individuals. After all, if you make loans to businesses and individuals, you run a risk. During the recession of 2007–2009, that risk appeared to be much greater than normal. Why not just sit back, collect interest checks from the U.S. government on all of your reserves, and wait to see what happens?

Well, that is exactly how most banks have proceeded over the past few years. The numbers tell the story. When they didn't earn interest, excess reserves were a drag on bank profits, and so banks kept them to a minimum. Typically, excess reserves for the entire banking system averaged $2–$3 billion. During 2011 they peaked at over $1.2 *trillion*, and since then have routinely been from $800 billion and up, depending on the day. Thus, most of the reserves injected into the banking system from 2008 to 2011 ended up not in new loans, new money, and new spending. Instead, they ended up sitting in the form of new excess reserves. That means that the "expansionary" quantitative easing of the Fed was almost completely offset by its decision to pay interest on excess reserves. The result was little increase in aggregate demand and little upward pressure on inflation—at least in the short run.

ON WANTING MORE INFLATION

For several years, the Fed has told reporters and experts alike that it was worried about **deflation.** (See Chapter 11.) Deflation has been associated with bad times—the Great Depression in the United States, for example, and the "lost decade" of the 1990s in the Japanese economy. In justification of its quantitative easing (QE2) in November 2010, the Fed pointed to the "need" for a little bit of inflation, to avoid a deflationary downward spiral.

Actually, as measured by the personal consumption expenditure price index, there had been inflation running at about 1.2 percent annually, a number that was bumping up around 2 percent toward the end of 2010 and into 2011. In other words, based on the Fed's historically preferred price index, there has been no sign of deflation, so it is strange that the Fed has argued in favor of quantitative easing to avoid deflation. The source of the Fed's deflation worries is easily identified, though. Without much publicity, in 2010 the Fed switched from the personal consumption expenditure price index to the consumer price index (CPI) as its preferred measure of inflation. The CPI gives almost double the weight to housing prices than does the personal consumption expenditure price index. Given that housing prices fell quite dramatically during the years 2006–2010, it is not surprising that the CPI has showed some deflation, especially in 2008.

GETTING BACK TO QUANTITATIVE EASING

Even if the Fed's argument about deflation is based on no more than a switch in price indexes, its desire to prime the pump for the faltering U.S. economy is genuine. The recession that started in December 2007 pushed the unemployment rate above 10 percent, and the rate was slow to drop back below 9 percent. So the Fed argued that QE2 would lower long-term interest rates and thereby give the economy a boost.

When the Fed buys up government and other debt obligations, it will push investors into stocks and corporate bonds—raising the latter's values and lowering interest rates. Lower borrowing costs should help some homeowners refinance their mortgages. Some businesses will be helped, too, because they will have access to cheaper credit. Such analysis is quite traditional and at times has worked—*in the short run*. In the long run, in contrast, large-scale purchases of debt, whether labeled quantitative easing or not, will simply lead to a higher rate of inflation and a return of interest rates to their previous and even higher levels.

So, the Fed might well be thought of as being on a tightrope of its own making. The huge infusion of reserves into the banking system helped moderate the recession of 2007–2009, but the payment of interest on reserves slowed the recovery from that recession. The presence of large excess reserves presents a huge potential threat of inflation down the road, but if the reserves are pulled out of the banking system too fast, the economy will surely sink back into recession. It is the classic case of the two-handed economic policy problem. On the one hand, the economy is threatened by severe inflation. On the other hand, it is threatened by a relapse into recession. Stay tuned, for this is one drama that will work itself out in front of your very eyes.

FOR CRITICAL ANALYSIS

1. Why do increases in the money supply in circulation ultimately lead to inflation?

2. Was the Fed justified in targeting specific sectors of the economy during the financial panic of 2008? Why or why not?

3. When the Fed buys U.S. government securities, how does it pay for them?

4. Is there any risk to the Fed in holding mortgage-backed securities and debt issued by Fannie Mae and Freddie Mac? If so, what is it?

5. Why did excess reserves increase so much in recent years?

6. Why have banks been so reluctant to loan funds to businesses in recent years?

CHAPTER **22**

Deposit Insurance and Financial Markets

During the Panic of '08, the federal government announced a key new policy: It was insuring against loss all bank deposits up to $250,000 per account. So if your depository institution happened to be holding some toxic (possibly even worthless) **mortgage-backed securities**, you were home free. The bank could suffer terrible losses, even go out of business, and yet your accounts, up to $250,000 each, would be guaranteed by the full faith and of the U.S. government—which is to say, the U.S. taxpayer.

If you happened to notice the announcement of this policy, you may have wondered to yourself, why would the government do this? For example, although the federal government bought **shares of stock** in numerous banks at the same time, it most assuredly does not guarantee the value of those shares. Why treat deposits differently? A more subtle question is this: How do banks and other **depository institutions** behave differently because of this special deposit insurance? And you might even have wondered whether *your* behavior is likely to be any different because of this insurance. To get a handle on these and other questions, we must look back to the 1930s, before the notion of deposit insurance had even been conceived.

Runs on Banks

Bank runs are defined as the simultaneous rush of depositors to convert their deposits into **currency.** Until the federal government set up deposit insurance in 1933, runs on banks were an infrequent but seemingly unavoidable occurrence, sometimes becoming widespread during economic **recessions.** The largest number of bank runs in modern history occurred during the Great Depression. As a result, more than *nine thousand* banks failed during the 1930s.

Just put yourself in the shoes of the depositor in a typical bank in 1930 and remember that you are a **creditor** of the bank. That is to say, your deposits in the bank are its **liabilities.** Suppose a rumor develops that the **assets** of the bank are not sufficient to cover its liabilities. In other words, the bank is, or will soon be, **insolvent.** Presumably, you are worried that you won't get your deposits back in the form of currency. Knowing this, you are likely to rush to the bank. All other depositors who hear about the bank's supposedly weak financial condition are likely to do the same thing.

This is the essence of a bank run: Regardless of the true state of the bank's financial condition, rumors or fears that a bank is in trouble can cause depositors to suddenly attempt to withdraw all of their funds. But many assets of a bank are in the form of loans that cannot immediately be converted into cash. Even if solvent, the bank is said to be **illiquid** because it doesn't have enough cash on hand to meet the demands of fearful depositors. And when it attempts to get that cash by selling some assets, any resulting decline in the market value of those assets can quickly turn a **solvent** bank into an insolvent one.

Bank runs can be disastrous for the economy because when they occur, the nation's **money supply** shrinks as people pull cash out of banks and stuff it under their mattresses (or wherever they think it might be safe). This in turn causes **aggregate demand** to fall, leading to higher unemployment, business failures, and yet more concerns for the solvency of banks. Quickly enough, the result can be an economic recession and widespread hardship.

DEPOSIT INSURANCE

When bank failures hit four thousand in 1933, the federal government decided to act to prevent further bank runs. That year, Congress passed, and the president signed into law, legislation creating the Federal Deposit Insurance Corporation (FDIC) and the next year created the Federal Savings and Loan Insurance Corporation (FSLIC). Many years later, in 1971, the National Credit Union Share Insurance Fund (NCUSIF) was created to insure credit union deposits, and in 1989, the FSLIC was replaced by the Savings Association Insurance Fund (SAIF). To make our discussion simple, we will focus only on the FDIC, but the general principles apply to all of these agencies.

When the FDIC was formed, it insured each account in a commercial bank against a loss of up to $2,500. That figure has been increased on seven different occasions, reaching $250,000 in 2008. The result of federal deposit insurance is that there has not been a widespread bank run in the United States since the Great Depression, despite numerous bank failures in the interim. Even during the Panic of 2008, when confidence in many financial institutions collapsed, federally insured depository institutions continued to operate. Indeed, total deposits in them actually rose. The good news about federal deposit insurance is that it has prevented bank runs. But this has come at a significant cost, arising largely due to the unintended consequences of deposit insurance.

Adverse Selection

Suppose someone offers you what is claimed to be a great **investment** opportunity. That person tells you that if you invest $250,000, you will make a very high rate of return, say, 20 percent per year, much higher than the 3 percent your funds are currently earning elsewhere. No matter how much you trusted the person offering you this deal, you would probably do some serious investigation of the proposed investment before you handed over fifty thousand hard-earned dollars. You, like other people, would carefully evaluate the risk factors involved in this potential opportunity.

For example, if you use part of your **savings** to buy a house, you will undoubtedly have the structural aspects of the house checked out by an inspector before you sign on the dotted line. Similarly, if you planned to purchase an expensive piece of art, you surely would have an independent expert verify that the artwork is authentic. Typically, the same is true every time you place your accumulated savings into any potential investment: You look before you leap. In circumstances such as these, there is initially **asymmetric information**—in this case, the seller knows much more than the potential buyer. But with diligence, the buyer can eliminate much of this gap in knowledge and make a wise decision.

Now ask yourself, when is the last time you examined the financial condition or lending activities of the depository institution at which you have your checking or savings account? We predict that the answer is never. Indeed, why should you investigate? Because of federal deposit insurance, you know that even if the depository institution that has your funds is taking big risks, you are personally risking nothing. If that depository institution fails, the federal government will—with 100 percent certainty—make sure that you get 100 percent of your deposits back, up to the insurance limit.

So here we have it, the first unintended consequence of depository insurance. Depositors like you no longer have any substantial incentive to investigate the track record of the owners or managers of banks. You care little about whether they have a history of risky or imprudent behavior because at worst you may suffer some minor inconvenience if your bank fails. So unlike in the days before deposit insurance, the marketplace today does little to monitor or punish past performance of owners or managers of depository institutions. As a result, we tend to get **adverse selection**—instead of banks owned and operated by individuals who are prudent at making careful decisions on behalf of depositors, many of them end up run by people who have a high tolerance for taking big risks with other people's money.

MORAL HAZARD

Now let's look at bank managers' incentives to act cautiously when making loans. You must first note that the riskier the loan, the higher the interest rate that a bank can charge. For example, if a developing country with a blemished track record in paying its debts wishes to borrow from a U.S. depository institution, that country will have to pay a much higher interest rate than a less risky debtor. The same is true when a risky company comes looking for a loan: If it gets one at all, it will be at a higher-than-average interest rate.

When trying to decide which loan applicants should receive funds, bank managers must weigh the trade-off between risk and return. Poor credit risks offer high **profits** if they actually pay off their debts, but good credit risks are more likely to pay off their debts. The right choice means higher profits for the bank and likely higher salaries and promotions for the managers. The wrong choice means losses and perhaps insolvency for the bank and new, less desirable careers for the managers.

To understand how bank mangers' incentives are changed by deposit insurance—even for managers who otherwise would be prudent and conservative—consider two separate scenarios. In the first scenario, the bank manager is told to take $250,000 of depositors' funds to Las Vegas. The rules of the game are that the manager can bet however he or she wants, and the bank will *share* the winnings *and losses* equally with the deposit holders whose funds the manager has in trust. In the second scenario, the same bank manager with the same funds is given a different set of rules. In this case, the bank doesn't have to share in any of the losses, but it will share in any of the gains when betting in Las Vegas.

Under which set of rules do you think the bank manager will take the higher risks while betting in Las Vegas? Clearly, the manager will take higher risks in the second scenario because the bank will not suffer at all if the manager loses the entire $250,000. Yet if the manager hits it big, say, by placing a successful bet on double zero in roulette, the bank will share the profits, and the manager is likely to get a raise and a promotion.

Well, the second scenario is exactly the one facing the managers of federally insured depository institutions. If they make risky loans, thereby earning, at least in the short run, higher profits, they share in the "winnings." The result for them is higher salaries. If, by contrast, some of these risky loans are not repaid, what is the likely outcome? The bank's losses are limited because the federal government (which is to say you, the taxpayer) will cover any shortfall between the bank's assets and its liabilities. Thus, federal deposit insurance means that banks get to enjoy all of the profits of risk without bearing all of the consequences of that risk.

So the second unintended consequence of deposit insurance is to encourage **moral hazard.** Specifically, bank managers of all types (risk lovers or not) have an incentive to take higher risks in their lending policies than they otherwise would. Indeed, when the economy turned down in the early 1980s, we got to see the consequences of exactly this change in incentives. From 1985 to the beginning of 1993, a total of 1,065 depository institutions failed, at an average rate of more than ten times that for the preceding 40 years. The losses from these failures totaled billions of dollars—paid for in large part by you, the taxpayer.

What, then, might be expected from the 2008 insurance hike to $250,000? Well, in the short run, confidence in banks was renewed and depositors were encouraged to keep more funds in banks. This was good news, for it helped the economy adjust to the financial shocks of 2008–2009. But the bad news will be forthcoming in the long run: The higher deposit insurance limits will encourage both adverse selection (more risk-loving bank managers) and moral hazard (more risk taking by bank managers of all stripes). Eventually, the lending standards of banks will deteriorate to the point that losses mount once again—paid for in part by you, the taxpayer.

Paying for Deposit Insurance

For the first 60 years or so of federal deposit insurance, all depository institutions were charged modest fees for their insurance coverage. Unfortunately, the fee that these depository institutions paid was completely unrelated to the riskiness of the loans they made. A bank that made loans to Microsoft was charged the same rate for deposit insurance as a bank that made loans to a start-up company with no track record whatsoever. Hence, not even the fees paid by banks for their insurance gave them any incentive to be prudent. This is completely unlike the case in private insurance markets, in which high-risk customers are charged higher premiums, giving them at least some incentive to become lower-risk customers.

In the early 1990s, the federal government made a feeble attempt to adjust fees for depository insurance to reflect the riskiness of their lending activities. But the political strength of the depository institutions prevented any fundamental change in the system. In 2008, the insurance fees paid by depository institutions were doubled, but even this was not enough to keep up with the added risks of the higher insurance limits. In 2009 the insurance rules were changed again. There are now four risk categories for banks, with different insurance premiums charged in each category. Although this is an improvement on the past, most experts believe that the system still not adequately charge banks for the risks they impose on the insurance system. That is, the premiums are not nearly enough to cover the likely losses of the riskiest banks or enough to get them to change their risky behavior.

So while your banker is headed to Vegas, you'd better plan on staying at home to work. Sooner or later, as a U.S. taxpayer, your bill for deposit insurance will come due.

FOR CRITICAL ANALYSIS

1. If federal deposit insurance costs nothing, who pays when an insured depository institution fails and its depositors are nonetheless reimbursed for the full amount of their deposits?

2. In a world without deposit insurance, what are some of the mechanisms that would arise to "punish" bank managers who acted irresponsibly? (*Hint:* There are similar types of mechanisms for consumer goods and in the stock market.)

3. Explain how "experience rating" of insurance—charging higher premiums to higher-risk customers—affects the incidence of both adverse selection and moral hazard.

4. Why doesn't the federal government fully price bank failure risks?

5. How would the chance of a major economic depression change if federal deposit insurance were eliminated?

6. Why doesn't the federal government offer automobile accident insurance?

CHAPTER 23

Credit Card Crunch

By the time you read this, you may already have had a credit card application denied or an existing card canceled. No, we are not talking about the credit card cutbacks that resulted from the recession of 2007–2009. We are referring to the effects of new **Federal Reserve** regulations (expanded by Congress) that are said to benefit you but have in many cases had exactly the opposite effect.

We speak of federal restrictions on the interest rates and fees that credit card firms may charge their customers. Since 2010, such firms are sharply limited in their ability to raise interest rates on existing credit balances, even if interest rates soar elsewhere in the economy. Moreover, the companies are limited in the fees they may charge customers who have little or no credit background or customers who have a troubled credit history. The result is a reduction in the credit available and credit that is more, not less, expensive to obtain.

Credit Card Complaints

If you have had a credit card for several years or know people who have, you have likely heard one or more "horror stories" about outrageous late fees or sky-high interest rates or other charges imposed by credit card companies. Some of these incidents are no doubt the result of unscrupulous practices by companies that prey on naïve consumers. Some companies have actually been able to commit fraud under the guise of being a credit card issuer.

But the vast majority of all credit cards are issued by companies that are in the business for the long haul. The interest rates and fees they charge are competitively determined and dependent on the (often substantial) risks of dealing with their cardholders. The practices of companies such as these are generally beyond reproach. Nevertheless, in 2008, the Fed and the other federal agencies that regulate credit card firms decided that the fly-by-night operators needed to be reined in. Congress got involved in 2009, passing legislation that buttressed the Fed's rules. Hence, a sweeping new series of regulations have been instituted, taking full effect in 2010. A positive result of the regulations is that some customers will be protected from fraudulent activities. Those elements of the new rules have proved beneficial to a limited set of consumers. But the new rules also severely hamper the way the *reputable* companies do business. The result of this has been less credit and more expensive credit—a lesson you may already have learned the hard way.

PRICE CONTROLS ON CREDIT CARDS

Among the myriad details of the new credit card regulations, the key provisions are those that limit the interest rates and fees that companies may lawfully charge. For example, firms are limited in the circumstances under which they can raise the interest rates they charge. Moreover, higher rates can only be applied to new charges, not to past balances— even if market interest rates in general have increased or the borrower has become a worse credit risk since the card was issued. Credit card firms are also limited in the fees they may charge when customers exceed their preset credit limits and the fees that they may charge for the subprime credit cards they issue to people with bad credit ratings.

As a practical matter, these provisions effectively act as **price controls**—legal limits on the prices that may be charged for goods or services. Here the controls are upper limits on prices, which means that interest rates and fees on credit cards are kept below their competitive levels. This causes firms' revenues to fall relative to their costs, which in turn reduces **profits** and discourages the firms from supplying the good in question, in this case consumer credit. On the other side of the market, because the legal maximum price is below the equilibrium price, people respond according to the law of **demand.** They try to obtain more of the good. In this case, consumers try to borrow more via credit cards. Because the quantity demanded rises and the quantity supplied falls, an excess quantity demanded is the result: People want to acquire far more than firms are willing to provide. In this case, desired borrowing goes up while desired lending goes down. Ultimately, the excess quantity demanded must be rationed somehow. The result is a series of readily predicted—and generally wasteful—consequences in the market. Let's see what those are.

LESS CREDIT

The first and foremost effect of the price controls is to reduce the amount of credit available to consumers. Firms have reduced the number of credit card offers they make, for example, because the expected profit from those cards is reduced by the limits on interest rates and fees. Many thousands of customers have had existing cards canceled because the new regulations made those cards unprofitable for the issuing companies. Credit card companies are also denying more consumer applications for credit cards because the firms are no longer able to cover the expected costs of issuing and servicing the cards of high-risk customers. And finally, when the companies do issue credit cards, they are generally imposing lower credit limits (maximum balances that consumers may have). This is because, for a customer with any given credit rating, the higher the credit balances, the higher the expected costs for the supplier of credit. Quite simply, as credit balances rise relative to a person's ability to pay, the chances rise that there will be late payments or no payments at all. Under the new rules, firms are less able to recoup those higher losses, so they have cut credit limits.

MORE EXPENSIVE CREDIT

Paradoxically, the net effect of limits on interest rates and fees has been to *raise* effective costs for many, perhaps most, customers. This is because the limits on interest rates and fees have reduced the amount of credit supplied and thus produced an excess quantity demanded, which, as we have noted, must be rationed somehow. To achieve this rationing, the cost to consumers of that credit must rise. There is simply no way to avoid this in a world of **scarcity.**

Some of these higher costs have come in the form of more onerous application procedures, which now require more documentation and verification. But there is another and even more important way that the cost of credit is driven up by the price controls on credit cards. Many people have been forced to turn to consumer finance companies, which typically charge interest rates of 30–40 percent per year, rather than the 15–30 percent routinely charged on credit card balances. In other instances, the new regulations have made life even worse than this for people with bad credit histories. Many of these individuals are now forced to obtain so-called payday loans.[1] These loans, usually made for

---

[1] One variant of these loans is sometimes called a "check into cash" transaction. Here is a simple example: The borrower receives $100 in cash today in return for writing the lender a personal check for $120, which the lender agrees not to cash until 2 weeks have passed. This deal translates into an implicit interest rate of about 10 percent *per week*.

one week to one month at a time, often carry interest rates as high as 500 percent per year! Thus, some of the people supposedly helped by the new regulations actually end up paying far more for their credit than they did before—as much as twenty times more.

THE POOR GET POORER

Of course, the developments of which we have spoken so far—reduced credit opportunities and higher credit costs—are not borne equally by all potential customers. In particular, affluent customers with top credit ratings have been essentially untouched. The fees and interest charges most affected by the new regulations are those that apply to people with poor credit ratings—generally, low-income individuals. As a result, it is these people, the ones supposedly helped, who are actually hurt the most. It is their applications that are being denied, and they are the ones turning to consumer finance companies and payday loan operations. For the well-to-do, it is business as usual. For the disadvantaged, it is one more example of a government regulation for which the principal consequences are "unintended," which is to say, directly contrary to the avowed purpose of the regulations.

WASTED RESOURCES

Not surprisingly, the new limits on interest rates and fees must be enforced, so the regulations have spurred growth in the bureaucracies of the Fed, the Office of Thrift Supervision, and the Federal Deposit Insurance Corporation. The credit card firms also face higher costs due to these regulations because they must demonstrate compliance with them and keep additional records. And because caps on rates and fees have forced the firms to conduct more credit checks and require more documentation, additional resources are being expended here. These are all resources that could have been put to good use elsewhere but are instead being used to implement and enforce the new price controls.

SAVERS LOSE TOO

Clearly, the new rules on interest rates and fees reduce the amount of credit extended to consumers. This means that the people who ultimately provide the funds for that credit lose too, because there is less demand for their savings. You might think that it is the credit card companies that are the ultimate source of those funds, but you would be wrong. In fact, it is ordinary savers who provide the funds that are lent to consumers by means of credit cards. The credit card companies merely act as intermediaries, moving the funds from savers to borrowers. Thus, people who have savings accounts or money market funds or small certificates of deposit are all now earning lower interest rates on their deposits because the interest rates paid by borrowers are controlled by the government.

THE BOTTOM LINE

The new price controls for credit cards have made the market less effective in allocating funds from savers to borrowers. As a result, our **wealth** as a society has been reduced. But at least the new rules enable us to see some key public policy principles in action:

There is no free lunch. It is nice to think that with the stroke of the regulatory pen, we might "make it so." But in a world of scarcity, that simply doesn't happen. Price controls distort incentives, raise costs, and reduce opportunities. Moreover, they are costly to implement and enforce, and they generally do not accomplish their avowed purpose, which is to help the disadvantaged.

People respond to incentives. When there is a reduction in the profits of making loans via credit cards, fewer of those loans are made. And when that happens, people have an incentive to turn elsewhere for funds. Even though those alternative sources are far more costly, they are not as costly for the borrowers as the option of doing without. And so people do what they must because they can no longer do what they wish.

Things aren't always what they seem. A superficial look at the credit market seems to suggest that people are better off because many of the people who do still have credit cards are paying lower interest and lower fees. But such a look misses the higher costs people are paying elsewhere and the losses that result because some people are unable to obtain any credit at all due to the new controls.

Policies always have unintended consequences, and so their net benefits are almost always lower than anticipated. Surely Congress and policymakers at the Fed didn't go into the regulatory process intending to reduce credit opportunities for low-income individuals. Nor did they hope to increase the credit costs that such individuals must actually bear to obtain credit under the new rules. But this is exactly what has happened, meaning that the rules produced fewer net benefits than the authors of the new rules intended.

So if you are one of the people who was turned down for a credit card, had one canceled, or was forced to turn to a higher-cost source of credit, there should be one consolation in all this: At least you have received an education in how the public policy process works in practice.

FOR CRITICAL ANALYSIS

1. Why do you suppose the government regulates interest rates on consumer credit (as with credit cards) but generally does not do so with commercial credit (as with loans to businesses)?

2. What do controls on interest rates do to the incentive of consumers to lie on their credit applications in an effort to qualify for a credit card?

3. More than 65,000 individuals and businesses submitted comments on the Fed's regulations when they were first proposed. How might a look at these comments (which are a matter of public record) help you identify individuals and businesses who are likely to gain or lose as a result of the regulations?

4. Why would a limit on interest rates on *old* credit card balances reduce the incentive of firms to issue *new* cards?

5. If government-imposed limits on interest rates are such a good idea, why not just make it illegal to charge *any* interest on *all* loans? What would be the consequences of such a policy?

6. The new limits on credit cards were imposed at a time that interest rates throughout the economy were at record-low levels. What will happen to the magnitude of the adverse effects of these limits as interest rates rise generally? Be explicit. Consider all of the adverse effects mentioned in this chapter. Who will be blamed for these consequences?

PART FIVE

Globalization and International Finance

CHAPTER 24

The Opposition to Globalization

The last 20 years has been a time of great change on the international trade front. The North American Free Trade Agreement (NAFTA), for example, substantially reduced **trade barriers** among citizens of Canada, the United States, and Mexico. On a global scale, the Uruguay Round of the General Agreement on Tariffs and Trade (GATT) was ratified by 117 nations including the United States. Under the terms of this agreement, the **World Trade Organization (WTO),** whose membership now numbers more than 150, replaced GATT, and **tariffs** were cut worldwide. Agricultural **subsidies** were also reduced, and patent protections were extended. The WTO has also established arbitration boards to settle international disputes over trade issues.

THE GAINS FROM TRADE

Many economists believe that both NAFTA and the agreements reached during the Uruguay Round were victories not only for free trade and **globalization** (the integration of national economies into an international economy) but also for the citizens of the participating nations. Nevertheless, many noneconomists, particularly politicians, opposed these agreements, so it is important to understand what is beneficial about NAFTA, the Uruguay Round, the WTO, and free trade and globalization.

Voluntary trade creates new **wealth.** In voluntary trade, both parties in an exchange gain. They give up something of lesser value to them in return for something of greater value to them. In this sense, exchanges are always unequal. But it is this unequal nature of exchange that is the source of the increased **productivity** and higher wealth that occur whenever trade takes place. When we engage in exchange, what we give up is worth less than what we get—if this were not true, we would not have traded. What is true for us is also true for our trading partner, meaning that the partner is better off, too. (Of course, sometimes after an exchange, you may believe that you were mistaken about the value of what you just received—this is called *buyer's remorse,* but it does not affect our discussion.)

Free trade encourages individuals to employ their abilities in the most productive manner possible and to exchange the fruits of their efforts. The **gains from trade** arise from one of the fundamental ideas in economics: A nation gains from doing what it can do best *relative to other nations,* that is, by specializing in those endeavors in which it has a **comparative advantage.** Trade encourages individuals and nations to discover ways to specialize so that they can become more productive and enjoy higher incomes. Increased productivity and the subsequent increase in the rate of **economic growth** are exactly what the signatories of the Uruguay Round and NAFTA sought—and are obtaining—by reducing trade barriers and thus increasing globalization.

KEEPING THE COMPETITION OUT

Despite the enormous gains from exchange, some people (sometimes a great many of them) routinely oppose free trade, particularly in the case of international trade. This opposition comes in many guises, but they all basically come down to one: When our borders are open to trade with other nations, this exposes some individuals and businesses in our nation to more **competition.** Most firms and workers hate competition, and who can blame them? After all, if a firm can keep competitors out, its **profits** are sure to stay the same or even rise. Also, if workers can prevent competition from other sources, they can enjoy higher wages and perhaps a larger selection of jobs. So the real source of most opposition to globalization is that the opponents of trade dislike the competition that comes with it. This position is not immoral or unethical, but it is not altruistic or noble, either. It is based on self-interest, pure and simple.

Opposition to globalization is nothing new, by the way. In the twentieth century, it culminated most famously in the Smoot–Hawley Tariff Act of 1930. This federal statute was a classic example of **protectionism**—an effort to protect a subset of U.S. producers at the expense of consumers and other producers. It included tariff schedules for over twenty thousand products, raising taxes on affected imports by an average of 52 percent.

The Smoot–Hawley Tariff Act encouraged so-called *beggar-thy-neighbor* policies by the rest of the world. Such policies are an attempt to improve (a portion of) one's domestic economy at the expense of foreign countries' economies. In this case, tariffs were imposed to discourage imports in the hope that domestic import-competing industries would benefit. France, the Netherlands, Switzerland, and the United Kingdom soon adopted beggar-thy-neighbor policies to counter the American ones. The result was a massive reduction in international trade. According to many economists, this caused a worldwide worsening of the Great Depression.

Opponents of globalization sometimes claim that beggar-thy-neighbor policies really do benefit the United States by protecting import-competing industries. In general, this claim is not correct. It is true that *some* Americans benefit from such policies, but two large groups of Americans lose. First, the purchasers of imports and import-competing goods suffer from the higher prices and reduced selection of goods and suppliers caused by tariffs and import **quotas.** Second, the decline in imports caused by protectionism also causes a decline in *exports,* thereby harming firms and workers in these industries. This result follows directly from one of the fundamental propositions in international trade: *In the long run, imports are paid for by exports.* This proposition simply states that when one country buys goods and services from the rest of the world (imports), the rest of the world eventually wants goods from that country (exports) in exchange. Given this fundamental proposition, a corollary becomes obvious: *Any restriction on imports leads to a reduction in exports.* Thus, any extra business for import-competing industries gained as a result of tariffs or quotas means at least as much business *lost* for exporting industries.

THE ARGUMENTS AGAINST GLOBALIZATION

Opponents of globalization often raise a variety of objections in their efforts to reduce it. For example, it is sometimes claimed that foreign companies engage in **dumping,** which is selling their goods in the United States "below cost." The first question to ask when such charges are made is, below *whose* cost? Clearly, if the foreign firm is selling in the United States, it must be offering the good for sale at a price that is at or below the costs of U.S. firms. Otherwise it could not induce Americans to buy it. But the ability of individuals or firms to obtain goods at lower cost is one of the *benefits* of free trade, not one of its harmful aspects.

What about claims that import sales are taking place at prices below the foreign company's costs? This amounts to arguing that the owners of the foreign company are voluntarily giving some of their wealth to us, namely, the difference between their costs and the (lower) price they charge us. It is possible, though unlikely, that they might wish to do this, perhaps because this could be the cheapest way of getting us to try a product that we would not otherwise purchase. But even supposing it is true, why would we want to refuse this gift? As a nation, we are richer if we accept it. Moreover, it is a gift that will be offered for only a short time. There is no point in selling at prices below cost unless the seller hopes to soon raise the price profitably above cost!

Another argument sometimes raised against globalization is that the goods are produced abroad using "unfair" labor practices (such as the use of child labor) or production processes that do not meet U.S. environmental standards. Such charges are sometimes true. But we must remember two things here. First, although we may find the use of child labor (or perhaps 60-hour workweeks with no overtime pay) objectionable, such practices were at one time commonplace in the United States. They were common here for the same reason they are currently practiced abroad. The people involved were (or are) too poor to do otherwise. Some families in developing nations cannot survive unless all family members contribute. As unfortunate as this situation is, if we insist on imposing our values and attitudes—shaped in part by our high wealth—on peoples whose wealth is far lower than ours, we run the risk of making them worse off even as we think we are helping them.

Similar considerations apply to environmental standards. Individuals' and nations' willingness to pay for environmental quality is very much shaped by their wealth. Environmental quality is a **normal good.** This means that people who are rich (such as Americans) want to consume more of it per capita than people who are poor. Insisting that other nations meet environmental standards that we find acceptable is much like insisting that they wear the clothes we wear, use the modes of transportation we prefer, and consume the foods we like. The few people who can afford it will indeed be living in the style to which we are accustomed, but most people in developing countries will not be able to afford anything like that style.

There is one important exception to this argument. When foreign air or water pollution is generated near enough to our borders (e.g., in Mexico or Canada) to cause harm to Americans, good public policy presumably dictates that we seek to treat that pollution as though it were being generated inside our borders.

Our point is not that foreign labor or environmental standards are, or should be, irrelevant to Americans. Instead, our point is that achieving high standards of either is costly, and trade restrictions are unlikely to be the most efficient or effective way to achieve them. Just as important, labor standards and environmental standards are all too often raised as smokescreens to hide the real motive: keeping the competition out.

WHY ARE ANTITRADE MEASURES PASSED?

If globalization is beneficial and restrictions on trade are generally harmful, how does legislation such as the Smoot–Hawley Tariff Act and other restrictions on international trade ever get passed? The explanation is that because foreign competition often affects a narrow and specific import-competing industry, such as textiles, shoes, or automobiles, trade restrictions are crafted to benefit a narrow, well-defined group of economic agents. For example, limits on imports of Japanese automobiles in the 1980s chiefly benefited workers and owners of the Big Three automakers in this country: General Motors, Ford, and Chrysler. Similarly, long-standing quotas that limit imports of sugar benefit the owners of a handful of large U.S. sugar producers. Because of the concentrated benefits that accrue when Congress votes in favor of trade restrictions, sufficient funds can be raised in those industries to aggressively lobby members of Congress to impose those restrictions.

The eventual reduction in exports that must follow is normally spread throughout all export industries. Consequently, no specific group of workers, managers, or shareholders in export industries will be motivated to contribute funds to lobby Congress to reduce international trade restrictions. Further, although consumers of imports and import-competing goods lose due to trade restrictions, they, too, are typically a diffuse group of individuals, none of whom will be greatly affected individually by any particular import restriction. This simultaneous existence of concentrated benefits and diffuse costs led Mark Twain to observe long ago that the free traders win the arguments but the **protectionists** win the votes.

Of course, the protectionists don't win *all* the votes—after all, about one-seventh of the U.S. economy is based on international trade. Despite the opposition to free trade that comes from many quarters, its benefits to the economy as a whole are so great that it is unthinkable that we might do away with international trade altogether. Both economic theory and empirical evidence clearly indicate that on balance, Americans will be better off with freer trade achieved through such developments as NAFTA and the WTO.

FOR CRITICAL ANALYSIS

1. For a number of years, Japanese automakers voluntarily limited the number of cars they exported to the United States. What effect do you think this had on Japanese imports of U.S. cars and U.S. exports of goods and services *other than* automobiles?

2. Until a few years ago, U.S. cars exported to Japan had the driver controls on the left side (as in the United States). The Japanese, however, drive on the left side of the road, so Japanese cars sold in Japan have the driver controls on the right side. Suppose the Japanese tried to sell their cars in the United States with the driver controls on the right side. What impact would this likely have on their sales in this country? Do you think the unwillingness of U.S. carmakers to put the driver controls on the "correct" side for exports to Japan had any effect on their sales of cars in that country?

3. Keeping in mind the key propositions of globalization outlined in this chapter, what is the likely impact of international trade restrictions on the following variables in the United States: employment, the **unemployment rate, real GDP,** and the **price level**? Explain your responses.

4. During the late 1980s and early 1990s, American automobile manufacturers greatly increased the quality of the cars they produced relative to the quality of the cars produced in other nations. What effect do you think this had on American imports of Japanese cars, Japanese imports of American cars, and American exports of goods and services other than automobiles?

5. The U.S. government subsidizes the export of U.S.-manufactured commercial aircraft. What effect do you think this policy has on American imports of foreign goods and American exports of products other than commercial aircraft? Explain.

6. Who bears the costs and enjoys the benefits of the subsidies mentioned in the previous question?

Chapter 25

The $750,000 Job

In even-numbered years, particularly years evenly divisible by four, politicians of all persuasions are apt to give long-winded speeches about the need to protect U.S. jobs from the evils of **globalization.** To accomplish this goal, we are encouraged to "buy American." If further encouragement is needed, we are told that if we do not voluntarily reduce the amount of imported goods we purchase, the government will impose (or make more onerous) **tariffs** (taxes) on imported goods or **quotas** (quantity restrictions) that physically limit imports. The objective of this exercise is to "save U.S. jobs."

Unlike African elephants or blue whales, U.S. jobs are in no danger of becoming extinct. There are virtually an unlimited number of potential jobs in the U.S. economy, and there always will be. Some of these jobs are not very pleasant, and many others do not pay very well, but there will always be employment of some sort as long as there is **scarcity.** So when a steelworker making $72,000 per year says that imports of foreign steel should be reduced to save his job, what he really means is this: He wants to be protected from **competition** so that he can continue his present employment at the same or a higher salary rather than move to a different job that has less desirable working conditions or pays less. There is nothing wrong with the steelworker's goal (better working conditions and higher pay), but it has nothing to do with "saving jobs."

The Gains from Globalization

In any discussion of the consequences of international trade restrictions, it is essential to remember two facts. First, *we pay for imports with exports*. It is true that in the short run, we can sell off **assets** or borrow from abroad if we happen to import more goods and services than we export. But we have only a finite amount of assets to sell, and foreigners will not wait forever for us to pay our bills. Ultimately, our accounts can be settled only if we *provide* (export) goods and services to the trading partners from whom we *purchase* (import) goods and services. Trade, after all, involves a quid pro quo (literally, "something for something").

The second point to remember is that *voluntary trade is mutually beneficial to the trading partners.* If we restrict international trade, we reduce those benefits, both for our trading partners and for ourselves. One way these reduced benefits are manifested is in the form of curtailed employment opportunities for workers. The reasoning is simple. Other countries will buy our goods only if they can market theirs because they, too, have to export goods to pay for their imports. Thus, any U.S. restrictions on imports to this country—via tariffs, quotas, or other means—ultimately cause a reduction in our exports because other countries will be unable to pay for our goods. This implies that import restrictions must inevitably decrease the size of our export sector. So imposing trade restrictions to save jobs in import-competing industries has the effect of costing jobs in export industries. Most studies have shown that the net effect seems to be reduced employment overall.

THE ADVERSE EFFECTS OF TRADE RESTRICTIONS

Just as important, import restrictions impose costs on U.S. consumers as a whole. By reducing competition from abroad, quotas, tariffs, and other trade restraints push up the prices of foreign goods and enable U.S. producers to hike their own prices. Perhaps the best-documented example of this effect is found in the automobile industry, where "voluntary" restrictions on Japanese imports were in place for more than a decade.

Due in part to the enhanced quality of imported cars, sales of domestically produced automobiles fell from nine million units in 1978 to an average of six million units per year between 1980 and 1982. Prof-its of U.S. automakers plummeted as well, and some incurred substantial losses. The automobile manufacturers' and autoworkers' unions de-manded protection from import competition. Politicians from automo-bile-producing states rallied to their cause. The result was a "voluntary" agreement by Japanese car companies (the most important competitors of U.S. firms) to restrict their U.S. sales to 1.68 million units per year. This agreement—which amounted to a quota, even though it never officially bore that name—began in April 1981 and continued well into the 1990s in various forms.

Robert W. Crandall, an economist with the Brookings Institution, estimated how much this voluntary trade restriction cost U.S. consumers in higher car prices. According to his estimates, the reduced supply of Japanese cars pushed their prices up by $2,000 per car, measured in 2011 dollars. The higher prices of Japanese imports in turn enabled domestic producers to hike their prices an average of $800 per car. The total tab in the first full year of the program was over $8 billion. Crandall also estimated that about twenty-six thousand jobs in automobile-related industries were protected by the voluntary import restrictions. Dividing $8 billion by twenty-six thousand jobs yields a cost to consumers of more than $300,000 *per year* for every job preserved in the automobile industry. U.S. consumers could have saved nearly $5 billion on their car purchases each year if instead of implicitly agreeing to import restrictions, they had simply given $100,000 in cash to every autoworker whose job was protected by the voluntary import restraints.

The same types of calculations have been made for other industries. Tariffs in the apparel industry were increased between 1977 and 1981, preserving the jobs of about 116,000 U.S. apparel workers at a cost of $45,000 per job each year. The cost of **protectionism** has been even higher in other industries. Jobs preserved in the glassware industry due to trade restrictions cost $200,000 apiece each year. In the maritime industry, the yearly cost of trade restriction is $290,000 per job. In the steel industry, the cost of protecting a job has been estimated at an astounding $750,000 per year. If free trade were permitted, each steelworker losing a job could be given a cash payment of half that amount each year, and consumers would still save a lot of **wealth.**

The Real Impact On Jobs

What is more, none of these cost studies has attempted to estimate the ultimate impact of import restrictions on the flow of exports, the number of workers who lose their jobs in the export sector, and thus total employment in the economy.

Remember that imports pay for exports and that our imports are the exports of our trading partners. So when imports to the United States are restricted, our trading partners will necessarily buy less of what *we* produce. The resulting decline in export sales means less employment in exporting industries. And the total reduction in trade leads to less employment for workers such as stevedores (who load and unload ships) and truck drivers (who carry goods to and from ports). On both counts—the overall cut in trade and the accompanying fall in exports—protectionism leads to employment declines that might not be obvious immediately. Some years ago, Congress tried to pass a "domestic-content" bill for automobiles. The legislation would have required that cars sold in the United States have a minimum percentage of their components manufactured and assembled in this country. Proponents of the legislation argued that it would have protected 300,000 jobs in the U.S. automobile manufacturing and auto parts supply industries. Yet the legislation's supporters failed to recognize the negative impact of the bill on trade in general and its ultimate impact on U.S. export industries. A U.S. Department of Labor study did recognize these impacts, estimating that the domestic-content legislation would have cost more jobs in trade-related and export industries than it protected in import-competing businesses. Congress ultimately decided not to impose a domestic-content requirement for cars sold in the United States.

THE LONG-RUN FAILURE OF IMPORT CONTROLS

In principle, trade restrictions are imposed to provide economic help to specific industries and to increase employment in those industries. Ironically, the long-term effects may be just the opposite. Researchers at the **World Trade Organization (WTO)** examined employment in three industries that have been heavily protected throughout the world: textiles, clothing, and iron and steel. Despite stringent **protectionist** measures, employment in these industries actually declined during the period of protection, in some cases dramatically. In textiles, employment fell 22 percent in the United States and 46 percent in the European Common Market (the predecessor of the **European Union**). Employment losses in the clothing industry ranged from 18 percent in the United States to 56 percent in Sweden. Losses in the iron and steel industry ranged from 10 percent in Canada to 54 percent in the United States. In short, the WTO researchers found that restrictions on free trade were no guarantee against employment losses, even in the industries supposedly being protected.

The evidence seems clear: The cost of protecting jobs in the short run is enormous, and in the long run, it appears that jobs cannot be protected, especially if one considers all aspects of protectionism. Free trade is a tough platform on which to run for office, but it is likely to be the one that will yield the most general benefits if implemented. Of course, this does not mean that politicians will embrace it. So we end up "saving jobs" at an annual cost of $750,000 each.

For Critical Analysis

1. If it would be cheaper to give each steelworker $375,000 per year in cash than impose restrictions on steel imports, why do we have the import restrictions rather than the cash payments?

2. Most U.S. imports and exports travel through our seaports at some point. How do you predict that members of Congress from coastal states would vote on proposals to restrict international trade? What other information would you want to know in making such a prediction?

3. Who gains and who loses from import restrictions? In answering, you should consider both consumers and producers in both the country that imposes the restrictions and in the other countries affected by them. Also, be sure to take into account the effects of import restrictions on *export* industries.

4. When you go shopping for a new computer, is your real objective to "import" a computer into your apartment, or is it to "export" cash from your wallet? What does this tell you about the true object of international trade—is it imports or exports?

5. Some U.S. policy is designed to subsidize exports and thus increase employment in export industries. What effect does such policy have on our imports of foreign goods and thus on employment in industries that compete with imports?

6. What motivates politicians to impose trade restrictions?

CHAPTER **26**

The Trade Deficit

The idea is not new. Indeed, it goes back centuries: Selling to foreigners is better than buying from them. That is, exports are good and imports are bad. Today, reading between the lines of the press coverage about international trade reveals that political and public thinking is not much different than it was three hundred years ago. The **mercantilists** who ruled public policy during the sixteenth through eighteenth centuries felt that the only proper objective of international trade was to expand exports without expanding imports. Their goal was to acquire large amounts of the gold that served as the money of their era. The mercantilists felt that a **trade surplus** (an excess of goods and service exports over imports) was the only way a nation could gain from trade. This same idea is expressed by modern-day patriots who reason, "If I buy a Sony laptop computer from Japan, I have the laptop and Japan has the money. On the other hand, if I buy a Dell laptop in the United States, I have the laptop and the United States has the money. I should therefore 'buy American.'" This sort of reasoning leads to the conclusion that the persistent international **trade deficit** that the United States experiences year after year is bad for America. Let's see if this conclusion makes any sense.

MODERN-DAY MERCANTILISTS

During any given month, you cannot fail to see headlines about our continuing (or growing) trade deficit. Even if you are not quite sure how to calculate our international trade deficit, you might guess that the problem seems to be that we are importing more than we are exporting.

Table 26-1 Exports and Imports of Goods (Billions of Dollars)

Year	Exports	Imports	Deficit
2000	772.0	−1,224.4	−452.4
2001	718.7	−1,145.9	−427.2
2002	682.4	−1,164.7	−482.3
2003	713.4	−1,260.7	−547.3
2004	807.5	−1,472.9	−665.4
2005	894.6	−1,677.4	−782.8
2006	1,023.1	−1,861.4	−838.3
2007	1,160.4	−1,983.1	−823.2
2008	1,304.9	−2,139.5	−834.7
2009	1,068.5	−1,575.4	−506.9
2010	1,288.7	−1935.7	−647.1

Source: U.S. Department of Commerce, Bureau of Economic Analysis.

Note: Sums may not add to totals due to rounding.

To understand the actual numbers reported in the press, you must understand that there are several components of trade deficits. The most obvious part consists of merchandise exports and imports. This is the number that receives the most coverage in the press. Table 26–1 shows the merchandise (goods) trade deficit for the United States for a recent ten-year period.

It looks pretty bad, doesn't it? It seems as if we've become addicted to imports. But merchandise is not the only thing that we buy and sell abroad. Increasingly, service exports and imports are a major component of international trade, at least in the United States. (Some of the types of services we export involve accounting, legal research, investment advice, travel and transportation, and medical research.) For these and other service items, even mercantilists would be happy to know that the United States consistently exports more than it imports, as you can see in Table 26–2, which shows the *net* balance of trade for the various categories of services.

THE LINK BETWEEN IMPORTS AND EXPORTS

Obviously, a comparison of the two tables still shows a substantial trade deficit, no matter how many times you look at the numbers. Should residents of the United States be worried? Before we can answer this question, we must look at some basic propositions about the relationship between imports and exports.

Table 26–2 Net Exports of Services (Billions of Dollars)

Year	Net Service Exports
2000	74.9
2001	64.4
2002	61.2
2003	52.4
2004	54.1
2005	66.0
2006	85.0
2007	119.1
2008	135.9
2009	132.0
2010	151.3

Source: U.S. Department of Commerce, Bureau of Economic Analysis.

We begin by considering how we pay for the foreign goods and services that we import. Countries do not ship goods to the United States simply to hold pieces of paper in exchange. Businesses in the rest of the world ship us goods and services because they want goods and services in exchange. That means only one thing, then: *In the long run, we pay for imports with exports. So in the long run, imports must equal exports.* The short run is a different story, of course. Imports can be paid for by the sale of real and financial **assets,** such as land, **shares of stock,** and **bonds,** or through an extension of credit from other countries. But in the long run, foreigners eventually want goods and services in return for the goods and services they send us. **Consumption** is, after all, the ultimate objective of production.

Because imports are paid for with exports in the long run, any attempt to reduce this country's trade deficit by restricting imports must also affect exports. In fact, a direct corollary of our first proposition must be that *any restrictions on imports must ultimately lead to a reduction in exports.* Thus, every time politicians call for a reduction in our trade deficit, they are implicitly calling for a reduction in exports, at least in the long run.

It is possible that politicians don't understand this, but even if they did, they might still call for restricting imports. After all, it is easy for the domestic firms that lose business to foreign competition to claim that every dollar of imports represents a lost dollar of sales for them— implying a corresponding reduction in U.S. employment. In contrast, the tens of thousands of exporters of U.S. goods and services probably won't ever be able to put an exact value on their reduced sales and employment due to proposed and actual import restrictions. Hence, the people with "evidence" about the supposed harms of imports will always outnumber those businesses who lose export sales when international trade is restricted.

A RENEGADE VIEW OF IMPORTS?

Many discussions about international trade have to do with the supposed "unfairness" of imports. Somehow, it is argued, when goods come in from a foreign land, the result is unfair to the firms and workers who must compete with those imports. To see how such reasoning is no reasoning at all, one need only consider a simple example.

Assume that you have just discovered a way to produce textiles at one-tenth the cost of your closest competitors, who are located in South Carolina. You set up your base of operations in Florida and start selling your textiles at lower prices than your South Carolina competitors do. Your workers are appreciative of their jobs, and your **shareholders** are appreciative of their profits. To be sure, the textile owners and employees in South Carolina may not be happy, but there is nothing legally they can do about it. This, of course, is the essence of unfettered trade among the fifty states: Production takes place where costs are lowest and consumers benefit from the lower prices that result.

Now let's assume that you build the same facility in Florida, but instead of actually producing the textiles yourself, you secretly have them brought from South Africa to sell, as before, at lower prices than those at which the South Carolina firms can profitably produce. If everyone continues to believe that you are producing the textiles on your own, there will be no problems. But if anybody finds out that you are importing the textiles, the political wrath of members of Congress from South Carolina will descend on you. They will try to prohibit the importation of "cheap" textiles from South Africa or put a high tax, or **tariff,** on those textiles.

Is there really any difference between these two "production processes"? The first one involves the use of some textile machinery within the United States, while the second involves having a ship and some trucks pick up the textiles and drop them off at the "factory" in Florida. Are they really any different? We think not. Such is the conclusion when using positive economic analysis. Once the world of politics gets involved, however, the domestic production process is favored and the production process that involves imports is frowned upon.

164 CHAPTER TWENTY SIX

THE OTHER SIDE OF TRADE DEFICITS

Most discussions of the trade deficit are further flawed by the fact that they completely ignore the mirror image of the deficit. In the short run, when exports of goods and services don't match up, dollar for dollar, with imports, the trading partners involved must obviously make arrangements for short-run methods to pay for the difference. For example, when the United States is importing more goods and services than it is exporting, we must be selling real and financial assets to our trading partners. For example, we might be borrowing from abroad (selling bonds) or selling shares of stock in U.S. corporations. (In the late 1990s, we also sold real estate, such as golf courses and office buildings.)

Now, at first blush, this sounds like we are "mortgaging the future," selling assets and borrowing funds in order to consume more now. But there is a different way to look at this: America is the safest, most productive place in the world to invest. *If the rest of the world is to be able to invest in the United States, we must run a trade deficit.* This proposition is a simple matter of arithmetic.

When, say, a South Korean automobile company builds a factory in the United States, there is an inflow of funds from South Korea to the United States. When foreign residents buy U.S. government securities, there is an inflow of funds from other countries to the United States. These investments are usually called *private capital flows,* and they include private land purchases, acquisitions of corporate stock shares, and purchases of government bonds. Virtually every year for at least thirty years, foreign residents have invested more in the United States than U.S. residents have invested abroad. This net inflow of capital funds from abroad is called a **capital account surplus.**

As a glance at Figure 26–1 reveals, this net inflow of investment funds into the United States nearly mirrors the trade deficit that the United States experiences each year. That is, when the current account trade deficit is small, the capital account surplus is small, and when the current account deficit is large, so is the capital account surplus. Is this just a coincidence? Certainly not. Think about it. If a foreign resident wants to buy stock in a U.S. company, that foreign resident must obtain dollars to pay for the stock. While it is true that the foreign resident simply goes to the foreign exchange market to do so, these dollars must somehow get supplied to the foreign exchange market. That supply of dollars must in turn come from the excess of U.S. goods and services imports over exports each year. In other words, *our international trade deficit supplies the dollars in foreign exchange markets necessary for foreigners to invest in the United States.* If Americans did not import more goods and services than they export, foreign residents could not invest in the United States.

Figure 26–1 The Relationship between the Current Account and the Capital Account.

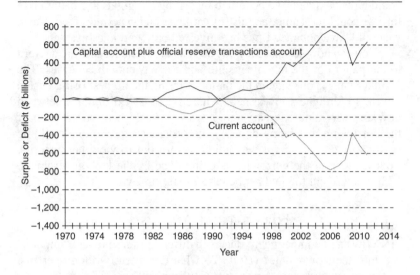

Sources: International Monetary Fund; *Economic Indicators*

THE SWEEP OF HISTORY

Contrary to what you might think from reading the newspapers, although the United States has been running a trade deficit for the past thirty-five years, this is not the first time we have run such a deficit over a long period of time. Indeed, from the Civil War to World War I, the United States ran a trade deficit year after year, borrowing funds and selling corporate stock all around the world. Were the consequences disastrous? Hardly. We used the funds we obtained from abroad to build railroads and steel mills and much of the rest of our industrial base, as well as to settle the West. We benefited from having access to low-cost finance (which we used to purchase key goods from abroad), and foreigners benefited from risk-adjusted rates of return that were higher than they could obtain in their home countries.

Beginning in World War I, this pattern reversed itself. Americans began lending money to Europeans to help them finance their war expenditures and then after the war lent them funds to rebuild. This pattern of American lending abroad continued through World War II and on until the late 1970s. All the while, we were running a trade surplus, exporting more goods and services than we were importing. Foreign residents were financing their purchases from us by borrowing and by selling us shares of stock in their corporations. They benefited by getting access to lower-cost finance and goods than they otherwise could have obtained. We benefited by selling our goods at a better price than we could get at home and also by earning a higher net rate of return than we could have obtained if we had invested only in domestic assets.

You can now see that the trade deficits of recent decades are a return to the pattern of the late nineteenth and early twentieth centuries. The United States is once again the nation offering the highest risk-adjusted return, so foreigners invest here. There is one key difference between now and one hundred years ago, however. Back then, virtually all of the borrowing was being done by the private sector, so one could be reasonably certain that it was going to turn out to yield net benefits. Today, much of the borrowing is being done by the U.S. government. Will this turn out to yield net benefits? Only time will tell.

FOR CRITICAL ANALYSIS

1. Why can't competing producers in different states prevent "imports" into their own state? (*Hint:* To what document written over two hundred years ago are the states still subject?)

2. How does the concept of "buy local" relate to concerns about trade deficits on an international basis?

3. Does it matter to you where the product you are buying has been manufactured? Why or why not?

4. What would have been the likely consequences for the development of the American economy between the Civil War and World War I if Congress has sought to reduce imports by, say, imposing high import tariffs? Explain.

5. In the three decades after World War II, Europe rebuilt from the war by borrowing from the United States and also by running a trade deficit with us. What would have happened to the rebuilding effort if European politicians had sought to reduce their trade deficit with the United States by imposing high import tariffs on American goods? Explain.

6. Some politicians express concern about our trade deficit with specific nations. For example, twenty years ago they worried about our trade deficit with Japan. More recently they have expressed concern over our trade deficit with China. Is there any reason to believe that a trade deficit with any particular nation is of any particular importance? If South Carolina runs a trade deficit with Texas, is this cause for concern in either state? Explain.

CHAPTER 27

The Value of
the Dollar

When the euro was introduced in 1999, you could purchase one for $1.18. Three years later, when euro banknotes and coins began circulating as the monetary unit of most of the **European Union (EU),** the market price of the euro had fallen to $0.90. Since then, the euro's price has fluctuated between $0.86 and $1.70. This pattern of fluctuating prices is not unique to the euro. In a world of **flexible exchange rates,** the prices at which different **currencies** trade for each other are determined by the forces of world **demand** and **supply.** Thus, if the demand for euros rises, its price will rise, and if its demand falls, so too will its price. And what is true for the euro is just as true for the British pound sterling, the Japanese yen, and our very own U.S. dollar. As we shall see, these changes in market forces, and the resulting changes in **exchange rates,** play a key role in determining patterns of international trade.

SOME TERMINOLOGY

Although we referred to the dollar price of the euro, we could just as well have talked of the euro price of the dollar. Thus, if it takes $1.25 to purchase a euro, it must also be true that a dollar buys less than a euro. In fact, it buys exactly 1/1.25 euros in this example. That is, the euro price of the dollar is €0.80 (where € is the symbol for the euro). The exchange rate between the two currencies can be expressed either way, although in America people usually refer to the exchange rate as the dollar price of foreign currency, and so too shall we. In this example, the exchange rate between the dollar and the euro is thus $1.25.

You will also hear some people, especially journalists and politicians, talk about a "stronger" or "weaker" dollar, accompanied by pronouncements that one or the other condition is good for America. When people say the dollar has gotten "stronger," what they mean is that one dollar will buy more units of foreign currency than it used to. Hence, a reduction in the exchange rate from, say, $1.25 to $1.20 per euro amounts to a stronger dollar. Conversely, if the dollar price of the euro rises from $1.25 to $1.35, this would mean that the dollar was weaker because one dollar would buy fewer euros.

GOOD NEWS OR BAD?

Is a weaker dollar good news or bad? Like most value judgments (notice the words *good* and *bad*), the answer is in the eye of the beholder. Suppose the price of the euro rises from $1.25 to $1.50. We say that the dollar has gotten weaker relative to the euro because people must pay more dollars for each euro. Because American consumers must eventually come up with euros if they want to buy French wine or Italian pasta, when the euro becomes more expensive, European goods become more expensive for American consumers.[1] So from the perspective of American consumers, a weak dollar is bad news.

But producers in America may have a different view of the world. For example, automobile manufacturers with plants in America compete with manufacturers that have European facilities. When the dollar price of the euro rises, so does the dollar price of cars made in Europe. This induces some American consumers to "buy American," which is surely good news for the companies that receive their business. Similarly, recall that the *rise* in the price of the euro is equivalent to a *fall* in the price of the dollar. Such a move in the exchange rate makes American-made goods cheaper abroad. As a result, foreign consumers are also more likely to "buy American," again good news for the companies from whom they purchase. Thus, a weaker dollar encourages exports and discourages imports, but whether that is "good" or "bad" news is clearly a matter on which people might reasonably disagree.

Now, what about the consequences of a "stronger" dollar? When the dollar can buy more euros, this means it can also buy more European goods. This clearly benefits American consumers, so we conclude that they like a strong dollar. American producers, however, will have a different take on matters. They will lose business from American customers, who are now more likely to "buy European." In addition, people in the EU will now find American goods more expensive

---

1 Of course, consumers typically don't physically obtain the euros themselves, but the importers who bring the goods in on their behalf must certainly do so.

because the dollar is now more expensive. So they will buy fewer American goods and make more purchases at home. Thus, we conclude that a stronger dollar will encourage imports into America and discourage exports from America. Presumably, American consumers and producers will have much different opinions on whether this is good news or bad.

PURCHASING POWER PARITY

Of course, exchange rates don't just move around without cause. There are four well-established forces that play key roles in making them what they are. The first of these, which is by far the most important long-run determinant of exchange rates, is called **purchasing power parity (PPP)**. This principle simply states that the relative values of different currencies must ultimately reflect their **purchasing power** in their home countries.

To see how this works, let's consider the United States and Switzerland, which uses the Swiss franc as its currency. Over the past fifty years, the exchange rate between these two currencies has varied between roughly $0.25 and $1.15, that is, by a factor of more than four. In the 1960s, for example, the exchange rate was near the bottom end of that range, but it has followed a persistent rise until quite recently, albeit with some ups and downs along the way. The reason the Swiss franc rose in value relative to the U.S. dollar is simple: Typically, the **inflation** rate in Switzerland has been much lower than that in the United States. The amount of goods that American dollars would buy generally has been shrinking, so the Swiss demand for dollars has fallen, even as Americans have tried to unload their depreciating dollars for Swiss francs. Together these forces helped push the value of the Swiss franc up, and so the exchange rate rose, to $0.40, then $0.70, and then even above $1.00.

This process applies across all countries. When the **price level** rises in country A relative to the price level in country B, people in both nations will switch some of their purchases of goods from country A to country B. This will push down the value of A's currency and push up the value of B's currency. In fact, this tendency is so strong that it will continue until "parity" is reached. If A's price level *rises* 20 percent relative to B's price level, then A's currency ultimately will *fall* in value by 20 percent relative to B's currency. It may take a while for this adjustment to work out, and it may be temporarily masked by some of the forces we shall talk about next, but eventually it will happen.

Interest Rates

One key reason for wishing to acquire the currency of another nation is that you want to acquire goods produced in that nation. But there is another reason: You may wish to invest or to lend funds in that nation. For example, suppose you wanted to purchase **bonds** issued by a Canadian corporation. These would be denominated in Canadian dollars (C$), so you would first have to obtain those Canadian dollars before you could purchase the bonds. Given this, it should be apparent that one of the factors influencing your demand for Canadian dollars is the rate of return, or interest rate, on **investments** in Canada, compared to the interest rate on investments elsewhere. The simplest way of putting this is that if interest rates in Canada rise relative to interest rates in the United States, investors will want to move funds from the United States into Canada. That is, there will be a drop in the demand for U.S. dollars and a rise in the demand for Canadian dollars, and so the exchange rate will rise—you will have to give up more U.S. dollars to obtain one Canadian dollar. The U.S. dollar will have become "weaker" against the Canadian currency.

Note that the interest rates of which we speak are **real interest rates,** that is, adjusted for any expected inflation. If interest rates rise in Canada because of an increase in the expected inflation rate there, this hardly makes them more attractive to American, European, or Chinese investors. It simply neutralizes the effects of the higher expected inflation. Similarly, we must be careful to compare interest rates on obligations that have the same **default risk.** If the interest rate is high on bonds issued by a Canadian company that is in danger of **bankruptcy,** that higher interest rate simply compensates **bondholders** for the added default risk they face. It doesn't make those bonds unusually attractive to investors in the United States or elsewhere.

But as long as we are careful to adjust for expected inflation and risk, interest rate differentials can sometimes be quite useful in understanding events. For example, during the late nineteenth century, inflation- and risk-adjusted interest rates were higher in the United States than they were in Britain because America was rebuilding from the Civil War, settling the West, and industrializing at a rapid rate. All of these factors made America a productive place in which to invest. The higher rate of return in America made it attractive for British investors to lend funds to American firms, which in turn meant a higher demand for American dollars. As a result, the American dollar was more valuable on world markets than it otherwise would have been.

HARD CURRENCY

If you've ever visited a developing nation or a formerly Communist country, you may have heard people refer to "hard currency." You may even have had them insist you pay for your purchases not with the local currency but with American dollars or euros or even Swiss francs. The reasoning behind this insistence is simple.

In such countries, whatever the *current* state of economic and political affairs, the *future* state of both is often filled with great uncertainty. Perhaps the current government's political support is not too secure. Or there may be the simmering threat of a military-backed coup. Or maybe there is a suspicion that the national government won't be able to finance its future spending with conventional taxes. Should any of these eventualities be realized, the likely result is that the government will resort to printing money as a means of financing its activities, causing future high inflation that will devastate the purchasing power of the local currency. And because the exact timing and magnitude of this outcome are highly uncertain, so is the expected future value of the local currency.

To reduce their risk, people thus try to hold currencies whose value is unlikely to be subject to political vagaries—and these are currencies issued by strong democratic governments, such as those in the United States and the EU. This increases the demand for such currencies and thus tends to set their values in world markets higher than they otherwise would be. The reference to "hard currency" stems from the notion that the purchasing power of such currencies is as stable as a rock—which it is, compared to the local monies that people are trying to avoid holding.

BOEING AND THE BEATLES

The final key factor that helps determine exchange rates is quite simply the relative attractiveness of the goods produced in various nations. Consider the Boeing Corporation, long regarded as the maker of some of the best commercial jet planes in existence. Airlines all over the world purchase billions of dollars' worth of Boeing aircraft every year. To do this, they must acquire U.S. dollars, and their demand for dollars makes the value of the dollar on world markets higher than it otherwise would be.

Of course, the residents of foreign countries have been known to produce some nice products themselves. Many people feel that the best wines come from France, the best ties from Italy, and so forth. And then there are the Beatles, perhaps the most prolific and popular rock group ever, at least measured by worldwide sales of music. When the Beatles hit the music scene in the 1960s, millions of Americans wanted to acquire recordings of their songs. To do so, they first had to acquire pounds sterling (the money used in Britain). This increased the demand for pounds sterling and thus caused the dollar price of the pound to rise in foreign exchange markets. So the next time you are paying to download music of the British rock group Coldplay, you will know that your decision to buy their music has pushed the dollar price of the pound sterling up, even if just by the tiniest of amounts.

FOR CRITICAL ANALYSIS

1. Although the United Kingdom is a member of the EU, it does not use the euro as its monetary unit. Instead it uses the pound sterling. If the United Kingdom decided to switch from the pound to the euro, how might this decision affect the value of the euro in foreign exchange markets?

2. In an effort to discourage drug smugglers from using U.S. currency in major drug deals, the U.S. government refuses to issue currency in denominations greater than $100. How does this policy decision affect the demand for dollars and thus the exchange rate between the dollar and other currencies, such as the euro (which comes in denominations as big as €500)?

3. Sometimes national governments decide that they don't want their currencies to be any lower in value than they currently are. Explain how, if a country wants to raise the value of its currency in foreign exchange markets, it might use the following tools to do so:

   (a) Altering the rate of growth in its money supply, thus changing the current and expected inflation rate

   (b) Limiting the ability of citizens to invest in foreign nations

   (c) Imposing **tariffs or quotas** on imports

   (d) Subsidizing exports by domestic firms

4. From shortly after World War II to the early 1970s, the United States (like many countries) was on a system of fixed exchange rates. That is, the U.S. government pledged to take whatever actions were necessary to keep the value of the dollar fixed relative to other

currencies. Consider the emergence of the Beatles in the 1960s. What would the U.S. government have to do to prevent the value of the dollar from changing as a result? Alternatively, consider the introduction of the popular Boeing 707 in the 1950s. What would the U.S. government have to do to prevent the value of the dollar from changing as a result?

5. Why do politicians worry about whether the dollar is "strong" or "weak"?

6. What do you think happened to the value of the U.S. dollar when BMW (a German company) moved an important part of its manufacturing facilities to the United States some years ago? Explain.

Glossary

abject poverty: surviving on the equivalent of $1 or less of income per person per day

adjustable-rate mortgage (ARM): debt used to finance house purchases, the interest rate on which changes depending on current market conditions

adverse selection: a process in which "undesirable" (high-cost or high-risk) participants tend to dominate one side of a market, causing adverse effects for the other side; often results from *asymmetric information*

aggregate demand: the total value of all planned spending on goods and services by all economic entities in the economy

appropriations bills: legislation that determines the size of government discretionary spending

asset: any valuable good capable of yielding flows of income or services over time

asset-backed security (ABS): a bond that has other assets (such as home mortgages) as collateral

asymmetric information: a circumstance in which participants on one side of a market have more information than participants on the other side of the market; often results in adverse selection

average tax rate: total taxes divided by income

balance sheet: a written record of assets and liabilities

bank run: an attempt by many of a bank's depositors to convert checkable and savings deposits into currency because of a perceived fear for the bank's solvency

bankruptcy: a state of being legally declared unable to pay one's debts so that some or all of the indebtedness is legally wiped out by the courts

Bankruptcy Code: the set of federal laws and regulations governing the process of declaring bankruptcy

bond: a debt conferring the right to receive a specific series of money payments in the future

bondholders: the owners of government or corporate bonds

book value: asset valuations that are based on the original purchase price of the assets rather than current market values

bubble: an episode in which asset prices exceed their values based on economic fundamentals, as determined by real future profits or service flows

budget constraint: all of the possible combinations of goods that can be purchased at given prices and given income

budget deficit: the excess of government spending over government revenues during a given time period

business cycles: the ups and downs in overall business activity, evidenced by changes in GDP, employment, and the price level

capital account surplus: a net inflow of capital funds (loans and investments) into a nation

capital ratio: the value of assets divided by the value of debt

capital stock: the collection of productive assets that can be combined with other inputs, such as labor, to produce goods and services

cash flow: cash receipts minus cash payments

central bank: a banker's bank, usually a government institution that also serves as the country's treasury's bank; central banks normally regulate commercial banks

checkable deposits: accounts at depository institutions that are payable on demand, either by means of a check or by direct withdrawal, as through an automated teller machine (ATM)

civil law system: a legal system in which statutes passed by legislatures and executive decrees, rather than judicial decisions based on precedent, form the basis for most legal rules

collateral: assets that are forfeited in the event of default on an obligation

collateralized debt obligation (CDO): an obligation to pay that is guaranteed by the pledge of another asset

commercial bank: a financial institution that accepts demand deposits, makes loans, and provides other financial services to the public

common law system: a legal system in which judicial decisions based on precedent, rather than executive decrees or statutes passed by legislatures, form the basis for most legal rules

comparative advantage: the ability to produce a good or service at a lower opportunity cost compared to other producers

constant-quality price: price adjusted for any change in the quality of the good or service

consumer price index (CPI): a measure of the dollar cost of purchasing a bundle of goods and services assumed to be representative of the consumption pattern of a typical consumer; one measure of the price level

consumption: spending by consumers on new goods and services

core inflation: a measure of the overall rate of change in prices of goods, excluding energy and food

cost of living: the dollar cost (relative to a base year) of achieving a given level of satisfaction

creative destruction: the ultimate outcome of a competitive process in which innovation continually creates new products and firms and replaces existing firms and products

credit-default swap: a financial contract in which the buyer of the swap makes a series of payments to the seller, who agrees to makes a pay-off to the buyer if an underlying financial instrument (such as a bond) goes into default

creditor: an institution or individual that is owed money by another institution or individual

currency: paper money and coins issued by the government to serve as a medium of exchange

default: failure to meet obligations, for example, the failure to make debt payments

default risk: an estimation combining the probability that a contract will not be adhered to and the magnitude of the loss that will occur if it is not

deficit: excess of government spending over tax receipts during a given fiscal year

deflation: a decline in the average level of the prices of goods and services

deindustrialization: a process of social and economic change caused by the removal or reduction of industrial capacity or activity in a country or region

demand: the willingness and ability to purchase goods

depository institutions: financial institutions that accept deposits from savers and lend those deposits out to borrowers

depression: a severe recession

direct foreign investment: resources provided to individuals and firms in a nation by individuals or firms located in other countries, often taking the form of foreign subsidiary or branch operations of a parent company

disability payments: cash payments made to persons whose physical or mental disabilities prevent them from working

discouraged workers: persons who have dropped out of the labor force because they are unable to find suitable work

discretionary spending: government spending that is decided on anew
each year, rather than being determined by a formula or set of rules
disposable income: income remaining after all taxes, retirement contributions, and the like are deducted
dividends: payments made by a corporation to owners of shares of its
stock, generally based on the corporation's profits
drift: the average annual rate at which stock prices change over a long
period of time
dumping: the sale of goods in a foreign country at a price below the
market price charged for the same goods in the domestic market or at
a price below the cost of production
dynamic economic analysis: a mode of analysis that recognizes that
people respond to changes in incentives and that takes these responses
into account when evaluating the effects of policies
Earned Income Tax Credit: a federal tax program that permits negative
taxes, that is, that provides for payments to people (instead of collecting taxes from them) if their incomes go below a predetermined level
economic growth: sustained increases in real per capita income
elasticity: a measure of the responsiveness of one variable to a change
in another variable
entitlement programs: government programs for which spending is
determined chiefly by formulas or rules that specify who is eligible
for funds and how much they may receive
equity: assets minus liabilities; net asset value
European Central Bank (ECB): the central bank for the group of nations that use the euro as their monetary unit
European Union (EU): a supranational entity resulting from an agreement among European nations to closely integrate the economic,
political, and legal systems of the twenty-seven individual member
nations
excess reserves: funds kept on hand by commercial banks to meet the
transactions demands of customers and to serve as precautionary
sources of funds in the event of a bank run; may be held as vault cash
or as deposits at the Fed
exchange rate: the price of a currency expressed in terms of another
currency
expansion: a period in which economic activity, measured by industrial
production, employment, real income, and wholesale and retail sales,
is growing on a sustained basis
expansive monetary policy: actions that tend to increase the level or
rate of growth of the money supply

expected rate of inflation: the rate at which the average level of prices of goods and services is expected to rise

face value: the denomination in terms of a unit of account expressed on a coin or unit of currency

fair-value accounting: an accounting method in which the reported values of assets are adjusted to reflect (estimates of) the current market values of those assets rather than their purchase prices or their stated maturity value

Fannie Mae: U.S. government–sponsored enterprise established in 1938 to facilitate the market in home mortgages

federal budget deficit: the excess of the national government's spending over its receipts

federal funds rate: the nominal interest rate at which banks can borrow reserves from one another

Federal Reserve System (the Fed): the central bank of the United States

fiscal policy: discretionary changes in government spending or taxes that alter the overall state of the economy, including employment, investment, and output

fiscal year: the accounting year used by a government or business; for the federal government, the fiscal year runs from October 1 to September 30

flexible exchange rates: exchange rates that are free to move in response to market forces

foreclosure: the legal process by which a borrower in default under a mortgage is deprived of his or her interest in the mortgaged property

Freddie Mac: U.S. government–sponsored enterprise established in 1970 to facilitate the market in home mortgages

fully funded pension liability: an obligation to make postretirement contractual payment made to an individual that is guaranteed by a sufficient amount of assets as to make the payment virtually certain

gains from trade: the extent to which individuals, firms, or nations benefit from engaging in voluntary exchange

globalization: the integration of national economies into an international economy

government-sponsored enterprise (GSE): a federally chartered corporation that is privately owned, designed to provide a source of credit nationwide, and limited to servicing one economic sector

gross domestic product (GDP): the dollar value of all new, domestically produced final goods and services in an economy

gross public debt: all public debt, including that owned by agencies of the government issuing it

hedge funds: investment companies that require large initial deposits by investors and pursue high-risk investments in the hope of achieving high returns

human capital: the productive capacity of human beings

illiquid: when used in reference to a company or person—having insufficient cash on hand to meet current liabilities; when used in reference to an asset—that which cannot be easily and cheaply converted into cash

in-kind transfer: the provision of goods and services rather than cash, as in the case of Medicare, Medicaid, or subsidized housing

incentives: positive or negatives consequences of actions

income mobility: the tendency of people to move around in the income distribution over time

industrial policy: a set of government actions that attempt to influence which firms succeed and which fail

Industrial Revolution: the widespread radical socioeconomic changes that took place in England and many other nations beginning in the late eighteenth century, brought about when extensive mechanization of production systems resulted in a shift from home-based hand manufacturing to large-scale factory production

inefficient: an outcome that fails to maximize the value of a resource

inflation: a rise in the average level of the prices of goods and services

inflation tax: the decline in the real value or purchasing power of money balances due to inflation

inflationary premium: the additional premium, in percent per year, that people are willing to pay to have dollars sooner rather than later simply because inflation is expected in the future

inside information: valuable information about future economic performance that is not generally available to the public

insolvent: describing a financial condition in which the value of one's assets is less than the value of one's liabilities

insourcing: the use of domestic workers to perform a service traditionally done by foreign workers

institutions: the basic rules, customs, and practices of society

interagency borrowings: loans from one part of the federal government to another

interest group: a collection of individuals with common aims

intermediate goods: goods that contribute to present or future consumer welfare but are not direct sources of utility themselves; typically, they are used up in the production of final goods and services

investment: the creation of new machines, factories, and other assets that enable the production of more goods and services in the future

investment bank: a financial institution that helps companies or municipalities obtain financing by selling stocks or bonds on their behalf

investment security: a debt obligation for which the default risk is low

labor force: individuals aged 16 and over who either have jobs or are looking and available for work

labor supply curve: a schedule showing the quantity of labor supplied at each wage rate

liabilities: amounts owed; the legal claims against an individual or against an institution by those who are not owners of that institution

loophole: a provision of the tax code that enables a narrow group of beneficiaries to achieve a lower effective tax rate

lump sum tax rebates: fixed cash payments made by a government to taxpayers that are independent of taxpayer income

mandates: in the context of governments, regulations or laws that require other governments, private individuals, or firms to spend money to achieve goals specified by the government

margin: increment or decrement

marginal tax rate: the percentage of the last dollar earned that is paid in taxes

mark to market: an accounting practice in which the reported values of assets are adjusted to reflect (estimates of) the current market values of those assets rather than their purchase prices or their stated maturity value

median age: the age that separates the older half of the population from the younger half

median income: the income that separates the higher-income half of the population from the lower-income half

Medicaid: joint federal–state health insurance program for low-income individuals

Medicare: federal health insurance program for individuals aged 65 and above

medium of exchange: any asset that sellers will generally accept as payment **mercantilists**—believers in the doctrine of mercantilism, which asserted (among other things) that exports were the principal objective of international trade because they permitted the accumulation of gold

microeconomics: the study of decision making by consumers and by firms and of the market equilibria that result

monetary policy: the use of changes in the amount of money in circulation to affect interest rates, credit markets, inflation (or deflation), and unemployment

money supply: the sum of checkable deposits and currency in the hands of the public

moral hazard: the tendency of an entity insulated from risk to behave differently than it would behave if it were fully exposed to the risk

mortgage-backed security (MBS): a debt obligation that pledges home mortgages as collateral

mortgages: debts that are incurred to buy a house and provide that if the debt is not paid, the house can be sold by the creditor and the proceeds used to pay that debt

mutual funds: a pools of money that are invested in assets, often shares of stock in corporations

national debt: cumulative excess of federal spending over federal tax collections over time; total explicit indebtedness of the federal government

natural resource endowments: the collection of naturally occurring minerals (such as oil and iron ore) and living things (such as forests and fish stocks) that can be used to produce goods and services

negative tax: a payment from the government to an individual that is based on the individual's income

net public debt: the portion of the public debt that is owned outside of the government issuing it

net worth: the excess of assets over liabilities

nominal income: income expressed in terms of a monetary unit, such as the dollar

nominal interest rate: the premium, in percent per year, that people are willing to pay to have dollars sooner rather than later

nominal prices: the exchange value of goods, expressed in terms of a unit of account, such as the dollar or the euro

normal good: a good for which the demand increases as people's income or wealth grows

official, reported economy: commercial transactions on which taxes are paid, regulations are obeyed, required paperwork procedures being adhered to

open market: the market for U.S. Treasury securities

opportunity cost: the highest-valued, next-best alternative that must be sacrificed to obtain something

outsourcing: the use of labor in another country to perform service work traditionally done by domestic workers

pay-as-you-go system: a scheme in which current cash outflows are funded (paid for) with current cash inflows

payroll taxes: taxes that are levied on income specifically generated by workforce participation and that are generally earmarked for spending on specific programs, such as Social Security

per capita income: GDP divided by population

per capita real net public debt: net public debt, deflated by the price level and divided by the population

perfectly inelastic: having an elasticity (or responsiveness) of zero

permanent income: the sustained or average level of income that one expects will be observed over a long period of time

physical capital: the productive capacity of physical assets, such as buildings

price controls: government rules that limit the prices firms may charge for the goods or services they sell

price level: the average current-year cost, measured relative to the average base-year cost, of a typical basket of goods and services

productivity: output per unit of input

profits: the difference between revenue and cost

progressive tax system: a set of rules that result in the collection of a larger share of income as taxes when income rises

property and contract rights: legal rules governing the use and exchange of property and the enforceable agreements between people or businesses

proportional tax system: a set of rules that result in the collection of an unchanging share of income as income changes

protectionism: economic policy of promoting favored domestic industries through the use of high tariffs and quotas and other trade restrictions to reduce imports

protectionist: any attitude or policy that seeks to prevent foreigners from competing with domestic firms or individuals

public debt: the amount of money owed by a government to its creditors

purchasing power: a measure of the amount of goods and services that can be purchased with a given amount of money

purchasing power parity (PPP): the principle that the relative values of different currencies must reflect their purchasing power in their home countries

quantitative easing (QE): Federal Reserve policy that entails the purchase of various financial assets, conducted in an effort to increase aggregate demand

quota: a limit on the amount of a good that may be imported; generally used to reduce imports so as to protect the economic interests of domestic industries that compete with the imports

real gross domestic product (real GDP): the inflation-adjusted level of new, domestically produced final goods and services

real income: income adjusted for inflation; equivalently, income expressed in terms of goods and services

real interest rate: the premium, in percent per year, that people are willing to pay to have goods sooner rather than later

real per capita income (real GDP per capita): GDP corrected for inflation and divided by the population—a measure of the amount of new domestic production of final goods and services per person

real price: price of a good or service adjusted for inflation; equivalently, the price of a good or service expressed in terms of other goods and services; see *relative prices*

real purchasing power: the amount of goods and services that can be acquired with an asset whose value is expressed in terms of the monetary unit of account (such as the dollar)

real tax rate: share of GDP controlled by the government

real wages: wages adjusted for changes in the price level

recession: a decline in the level of overall business activity

regressive tax system: a set of rules that result in the collection of a smaller share of income as taxes when income rises

relative prices: prices of goods and services compared to the prices of other goods and services; costs of goods and services measured in terms of other commodities

required reserves: funds that a commercial bank must lawfully maintain; they may be held in the form of vault cash or deposits at the Fed

reserves: assets held by depository institutions, typically in the form of currency held at the institution or as non-interest-bearing deposits held at the central bank, to meet customers' transaction needs and Fed legal requirements

resources: any items capable of satisfying individuals' desires or preferences or suitable for transformation into such goods

revealed preferences: consumers' tastes as demonstrated by the choices they make

rule of law: the principle that relations between individuals, businesses, and the government are governed by explicit rules that apply to everyone in society

saving: an addition to wealth, conventionally measured as disposable personal income minus consumption

savings: one's stock of wealth at a given moment in time

scarcity: a state of the world in which there are limited resources but unlimited demands, implying that we must make choices among alternatives

securitized: describing cash flow–producing assets pooled and repackaged into securities that are then sold to investors

share of stock: claim to a specified portion of future net cash flows (or profits) of a corporation

shareholders: owners of shares of stock in a corporation

Social Security: the federal system that transfers income from current workers to current retirees

solvent: describing a financial condition in which the value of one's assets is greater than the value of one's liabilities

standard of living: a summary measure of the level of per capita material welfare, often measured by per capita real GDP

static economic analysis: a mode of analysis that assumes for simplicity that people do not change their behavior when incentives change

stock: as applied to measurement, an amount measured at a particular moment in time

stockbroker: a middleman who sells shares of stock to individuals

subprime mortgages: *mortgages* that entail the higher risk of loss for the lender

subsidies: government payments for the production of specific goods, generally intended to raise the profits of the firms producing those goods

supply: the willingness and ability to sell goods

systemic risk: hazard that is felt or experienced throughout an entire economy

tariff: a tax levied only on imports; generally used to reduce imports so as to protect the economic interests of domestic industries that compete with the imports

tax bracket: a range of income over which a specific marginal tax rate applies

tax credit: a direct reduction in tax liability, occasioned by a specific set of circumstances and not dependent on the taxpayer's tax bracket

tax evasion: the deliberate failure to pay taxes, usually by making a false report

tax liability: total tax obligation owed by a firm or individual

tax rate: the percentage of a dollar of income that must be paid in taxes

tax rebate: a return of some previously paid taxes

third party: in the context of health insurance, it is an entity other than the insured or the service provider that has a financial obligation in the transaction; typically an insurance company or government

trade barrier: a legal rule imposed by a nation that raises the costs of foreign firms seeking to sell goods in that nation; they include tariffs and quotas

trade deficit: an excess of the value of imports of goods and services over the value of the exports of goods and services

trade surplus: an excess of the value of exports of goods and services over the value of the imports of goods and services

Treasury bills: short-term notes of indebtedness of the U.S. government

underground economy: commercial transactions on which taxes and regulations are being avoided

unemployment benefits: regular cash payments made to individuals, contingent on their status as being unemployed

unemployment rate: the number of persons looking and available for work, divided by the labor force

unfunded pension liabilities: obligations to make postretirement contractual payment to individuals that are not guaranteed by a sufficient amount of assets as to make the payment virtually certain

unfunded taxpayer liabilities: obligations of taxpayers for which no specific debt instruments have been issued

voucher: a written authorization, exchangeable for cash or services

wealth: the present value of all current and future income

wealth tax: a tax based on a person's net worth

World Trade Organization (WTO): an association of more than 150 nations that helps reduce trade barriers among its members and handles international trade disputes among them

write off: declare to be worthless

Selected References
and Web Links

CHAPTER 1   Rich Nation, Poor Nation

Easterly, William, and Ross Levine. "Tropics, Germs, and Crops: How Endowments Influence Economic Development." *Journal of Monetary Economics* 50, no. 1 (2003): 3–39.

Mahoney, Paul G. "The Common Law and Economic Growth: Hayek Might Be Right." *Journal of Legal Studies* 30, no. 2 (2001): 503–525.

Rosenberg, Nathan, and L. E. Birdzell Jr. *How the West Grew Rich*. New York: Basic Books, 1987.

Spiers, Elizabeth. "The World's Worst Inflation." *Fortune*, August 18, 2008, p. 36.

www.worldbank.org. Official Web site of the World Bank.

CHAPTER 2   Going Underground

Barta, Patrick. "The Rise of the Underground Economy." *Wall Street Journal*, March 14–15, 2009, pp. W1–W2.

Caruso, David B. *In NYC, Cash and Connections Can Get You a Kidney*. Associated Press, August 20, 2009.

Embaye, Abel. *Underground Economy Estimates for Non-OECD Countries Using Currency Demand Method*. MPRA Paper no. 20308. January 2010.

Feige, Edgar L. *New Estimates of Overseas U.S. Currency Holdings, the Underground Economy, and the Tax Gap*. MPRA Paper no. 19564. December 2009.

CHAPTER 3   Outsourcing and Economic Growth

Council of Economic Advisers. *Economic Report of the President*. Washington, D.C.: Government Printing Office, 2004.

Garten, Jeffrey E. "Offshoring: You Ain't Seen Nothin' Yet." *Business Week*, June 21, 2004, p. 28.

Gnuschke, John E., Jeff Wallace, Dennis R. Wilson, and Stephen C. Smith. "Outsourcing Production and Jobs: Costs and Benefits." *Business Perspectives* 16, no. 2 (2004): 12–18.

Irwin, Douglas A. "Free-Trade Worriers." *Wall Street Journal*, August 9, 2004, p. A12.

Reinsdorf, Martin, and Matthew J. Slaughter (eds.). *International Trade in Services and Intangibles in the Era of Globalization*. National Bureau of Economic Research Studies in Income and Wealth, v. 69. Chicago, IL: University of Chicago Press, 2009.

CHAPTER 4   Poverty, Capitalism, and Growth

cia.gov/cia/publications/factbook. Central Intelligence Agency profiles of countries and territories.

Foundation for Teaching Economics. "Is Capitalism Good for the Poor?" (www.fte.org/capitalism/index.php)

Gwartney, James, Joshua Hall, and Robert Lawson. *Economic Freedom of the World: 2010 Annual Report*. Vancouver, Canada: Fraser Institute, 2010.

www.freetheworld.com. Fraser Institute site on economic freedom around the world.

CHAPTER 5   The Threat to Growth

Edwards, Chris. *Income Tax Rife with Complexity and Inefficiency*. Washington, D.C.: Cato Institute, 2006.

Goolsbee, Austan. "The Impact of the Corporate Income Tax: Evidence from State Organizational Form Data." *Journal of Public Economics* 88, no. 11 (2004): 2283–2299.

Harberger, Arnold C. "Three Basic Postulates for Applied Welfare Economics: An Interpretive Essay." *Journal of Economic Literature* 9, no. 3 (1971): 785–797.

Norton, Rob. "Corporate Taxation." *The Concise Encyclopedia of Economics*. (www.econlib.org/library/Enc/CorporateTaxation.html)

Rakowski, Eric. "Can Wealth Taxes Be Justified?" *Tax Law Review* 53, no. 3 (2000): 3–37.

CHAPTER 6   Is GDP What We Want?

"Grossly Distorted Picture." *Economist*, March 15, 2008, p. 92.

Steindel, Charles. "Chain Weighting: The New Approach to Measuring GDP." *Current Issues in Economics and Finance* 9, no. 1 (1995): 1–6.

Stevenson, Betsey, and Justin Wolfers. "Economic Growth and Subjective Well-Being: Reassessing the Easterlin Paradox." *Brookings Papers on Economic Activity*, Spring 2008, pp. 1–87.

bea.gov/bea/dn/home/gdp.htm. GDP data from U.S. Department of Commerce, Bureau of Economic Analysis.

CHAPTER 7   What's in a Word? Plenty, When It's the "R" Word

Business Cycle Dating Committee. "The NBER's Recession Dating Procedure." National Bureau of Economic Research, 2003. (nber.org/cycles/recessions.html)

Conference Board. "Business Cycle Indicators." (www.globalindicators.org)

Layton, Allan P., and Anirvan Banerji. "What Is a Recession? A Reprise." *Applied Economics* 35, no. 16 (2003): 1789–1797.

www.bea.doc.gov. Web site of the U.S. Department of Commerce's Bureau of Economic Analysis.

CHAPTER 8   The Great Recession

Calomiris, Charles W., and Peter J. Wallison. "Blame Fannie Mae and Congress for the Credit Mess." *Wall Street Journal*, September 23, 2008.

Friedman, Milton, and Anna J. Schwartz. *A Monetary History of the United States, 1867–1960*. Princeton, NJ: Princeton University Press, 1963.

Leibowitz, Stan J. *Anatomy of a Train Wreck: Causes of the Mortgage Meltdown*. Oakland, CA: Independent Institute, 2008.

Leonhardt, David. "Lesson from a Crisis: When Trust Vanishes, Worry." *New York Times*, October 1, 2008.

Nocera, Joe. "36 Hours of Alarm and Action as Crisis Spiraled." *New York Times*, October 2, 2008.

CHAPTER 9   The Case of the Disappearing Workers

Benjamin, Daniel K., and Kent G. P. Matthews. *U.S. and U.K. Unemployment between the Wars: A Doleful Story*. London: Institute for Economic Affairs, 1992.

Darby, Michael R. "Three-and-a-Half Million U.S. Employees Have Been Mislaid: Or, an Explanation of Unemployment, 1934–1941." *Journal of Political Economy* 84, no. 1 (1976): 1–16.

Wallis, John Joseph, and Daniel K. Benjamin. "Public Relief and Unemployment in the Great Depression." *Journal of Economic History* 41, no. 1 (1981): 97–102.

www.bls.gov. Web site of the U.S. Department of Labor's Bureau of Labor Statistics.

CHAPTER 10   Poverty, Wealth, and Equality

Becker, Gary S., and Richard A. Posner. "How to Make the Poor Poorer." *Wall Street Journal*, January 26, 2007, p. A11.

"Cheap and Cheerful." *Economist*, July 26, 2008, p. 90.

"Movin' On Up." *Wall Street Journal*, November 14, 2007.

U.S. Department of the Treasury. *Income Mobility in the U.S. from 1996 to 2005*. Washington, D.C.: Government Printing Office, 2007.

CHAPTER 11   Will It Be Inflation or Deflation?

Alchian, Armen A., and Reuben Kessel. "The Effects of Inflation." *Journal of Political Economy* 70, no. 6 (1962): 521–537.

Cagan, Phillip. "Monetary Dynamics of Hyperinflation." In *Studies in the Quantity Theory of Money*, ed. Milton Friedman. Chicago: University of Chicago Press, 1956.

Keynes, John Maynard. *The Economic Consequences of the Peace*. New York: Harcourt, Brace & Company, 1920.

Spiers, Elizabeth. "The Great Inflation Cover-Up." *Fortune*, April 14, 2008, pp. 25–26.

CHAPTER 12   Is It Real, or Is It Nominal?

Bresnahan, Timothy F., and Robert J. Gordon (eds.). *The Economics of New Goods*. NBER Studies in Income and Wealth no. 58. Chicago: University of Chicago Press, 1997.

Goklany, Indur M., and Jerry Taylor. "A Big Surprise on Gas." *Los Angeles Times*, August 11, 2008.

www.bls.gov. Web site of the Bureau of Labor Statistics, U.S. Department of Labor.

www.eia.doe.gov. Web site of the Energy Information Administration, U.S. Department of Energy.

CHAPTER 13   Are You Stimulated Yet?

Cogan, John F., and John B. Taylor. "The Obama Stimulus Impact? Zero." *Wall Street Journal*, December 9, 2010.

Friedman, Milton, and David Meiselman. "The Relative Stability of Monetary Velocity and the Investment Multiplier in the United States, 1897–1958." In *Commission on Money and Credit: Stabilization Policies*. Englewood Cliffs, NJ: Prentice-Hall, 1963, pp. 165–268.

Merrick, Amy. "Rejecting Stimulus, States Forgo Rail Funds." *Wall Street Journal*, December 10, 2010, p. A6.

Peltzman, Sam. "The Effect of Government Subsidies-In-Kind on Private Expenditures: The Case of Higher Education." *Journal of Political Economy* 81, no. 1 (1973): 1–27.

Saving, Jason. "Can the Nation Stimulate Its Way to Prosperity?" *Economics*. Letters—Insights from the Federal Reserve Bank of Dallas. 6, no. 8 (2010): 1–3.

CHAPTER 14   Health Care Reform

Cummings, N. A., and W. T. O'Donohue (eds.). *Understanding the Behavioral Healthcare Crisis: The Promise of Integrated Care and Diagnostic Reform*. Routledge Press, 2011.

Esmail, Nadeem. *Waiting Your Turn: Hospital Waiting Lists in Canada*, 19th ed. Vancouver: Fraser Institute, October 2009.

Hill, Brian E. *Stop the Noise: A Physician's Quest to Silence the Politics of Health Care Reform*. Santa Ana, CA: Griggen Publishing Group, 2010.

Mackey, John. "The Whole Foods Alternative to ObamaCare." *Wall Street Journal*, August 29, 2009, Opinion page.

Merion, Noel. *Health Care (Current Controversies)*. Cincinnati: Greenhaven Press, 2010.

Tanner, Michael. *Bad Medicine: A Guide to the Real Costs and Consequences of the New Health Care Law*. Cato Institute, 2010.

CHAPTER 15   The Fannie Mae, Freddie Mac Flimflam

Applebaum, Binyamin. "Cost of Seizing Fannie and Freddie Surges for Taxpayers." *New York Times*, June 10, 2010.

Berry, Kate. "When Taking on More Bad Loans Seems a Good Idea." *American Banker*, March 15, 2010.

Calomiris, Charles W., and Peter J. Wallison. "Blame Fannie Mae and Congress for the Credit Mess." *Wall Street Journal*, September 23, 2008.

Duhigg, Charles. "Pressured to Take on Risk, Fannie Hit a Tipping Point." *New York Times*, October 5, 2008.

Editorial Staff. "The Biggest Losers." *The Wall Street Journal*, January 4, 2010, p. A16.

Editorial Staff. "The Next Fannie Mae." *The Wall Street Journal*, August 10, 2009.

Wallison, Peter J. "The Price for Fannie and Freddie Keeps Going Up." *The Wall Street Journal*, December 30, 2009, p. A17.

CHAPTER 16 Big Bucks for Bailouts

Crain, Nicole V., and W. Mark Crain. "The Regulation Tax Keeps Growing." *Wall Street Journal*, September 27, 2010, Opinion.

Lerner, Josh. *Boulevard of Broken Dreams*. Princeton: Princeton University Press, 2009.

Schumpeter, Joseph A. *Capitalism, Socialism, and Democracy*. New York: Harper Perennial Modern Classics, November 2008 [originally published in 1942].

Utterback, James M. *Mastering the Dynamics of Innovation*. Cambridge: Harvard Business School Press, 1996.

CHAPTER 17 The Pension Crisis

Brainard, Keith. *Public Fund Survey Summary of Findings for FY2009*. National Association of State Retirement Administrators, October 2010.

Dugan, Ianthe Jeanne. "Facing Budget Gaps, Cities Sell Parking, Airports, Zoo." *Wall Street Journal*, August 23, 2010.

Fitch, Stephan. "Guilt-Edged Pensions." *Forbes*, February 16, 2009, pp. 79–84.

Malanga, Steve. "How States Hide Their Budget Deficits." *Wall Street Journal*, August 23, 2010.

The PEW Center of the States. *The Trillion Dollar Gap: Unfunded State Retirement Systems and the Roads to Reform*. Washington, D.C.: The PEW Charitable Trust, February 2010.

CHAPTER 18 Higher Taxes Are in Your Future

Council of Economic Advisers. *Economic Report of the President*. Washington, D.C.: Government Printing Office, 2011.

The 2010 Annual Report of the Board of Trustees of the Federal Old-Age and Survivors Insurance and Federal Disability Insurance Trust Funds. Washington, D.C.: Government Printing Office, 2008.

U.S. Office of Management and Budget. "Budget of the United States, Fiscal Year 2011." (www.whitehouse.gov/omb/budget)

www.brillig.com/debt_clock. One of many private Web sites that track the U.S. national debt.

CHAPTER 19 The Myths of Social Security

Congressional Budget Office. "Social Security: A Primer." September 2001. (www.cbo.gov/showdoc.cfm?index=3213&sequence=0)

Engelhardt, Gary V., and Jonathan Gruber. *Social Security and the Evolution of Elderly Poverty*. NBER Working Paper no. 10466. Boston: National Bureau of Economic Research, 2004.

Oshio, Takashi. *Social Security and Trust Fund Management*. NBER Working Paper no. 10444. Boston: National Bureau of Economic Research, 2004.

www.ssa.gov. Web site of the Social Security Administration.

CHAPTER 20 The Fed and Financial Panics

Friedman, Milton, and Anna J. Schwartz. *A Monetary History of the United States, 1867–1960*. Princeton, NJ: Princeton University Press, 1963.

Goodman, Peter. "Taking a Hard New Look at a Greenspan Legacy." *New York Times*, October 9, 2008.

Norris, Floyd. "Plan B: Flood Banks with Cash." *New York Times*, October 10, 2008.

CHAPTER 21 The Fed Feeding Frenzy

Guha, Krishna, and Tom Braithwaite. "Bernanke faces Senate grilling ion confirmation." *Financial Times*, December 2, 2009.

Hilsenrath, Jon. "After crisis, U.S. is set to rethink Fed's role." *Wall Street Journal*, May 18, 2009, p. A12.

Hilsenrarth, Jon, and Mark Whitehouse. "Markets Defy Fed's Bond-Buying Push." *Wall Street Journal*, December 9, 2010.

Lang, Jia Lynn, Neil Irwin, and David S. Hizenrath. "Fed Aid in Financial Crisis Went Beyond U.S. Banks to Industry, Foreign Firms." *Washington Post*, December 2, 2010.

CHAPTER 22 Deposit Insurance and Financial Markets

Allen, Franklin, and Douglas Gale. "Competition and Financial Stability." *Journal of Money, Credit and Banking* 36, no. 3 (2004): S453–S480.

Bordo, M., H. Rockoff, and A. Redish. "The U.S. Banking System from a Northern Exposure: Stability versus Efficiency." *Journal of Economic History* 54, no. 2 (1994): 325–341.

Diamond, D., and P. Dybvig. "Bank Runs, Deposit Insurance, and Liquidity." *Journal of Political Economy* 91, no. 3 (1983): 401–419.

Friedman, Milton, and Anna J. Schwartz. *A Monetary History of the United States, 1867–1960.* Princeton, NJ: Princeton University Press, 1963.

CHAPTER 23 Credit Card Crunch

Board of Governors of the Federal Reserve System. *Highlights of Final Rules regarding Credit Card Accounts.* December 18, 2008. (www.federalreserve.gov/newsevents/press/bcreg20081218a1.pdf)

Kaper, Stacy. "Fed Plans to Restrict Card-Rate Increase." *American Banker*, April 29, 2008.

Mcgrane, Victoria. "Major Provisions of the Financial Overhaul Bill." *The Wall Street Journal*, June 25, 2010.

Prater, Connie. "What the New Credit Card Reforms Mean for You." CreditCards.com, 2009. (www.creditcards.com/credit-card-news/what-the-new-credit-card-rules-mean-1282.php)

Silver-Greenberg, Jessica. "The New Credit-Card Tricks." *Wall Street Journal*, July 31, 2010.

CHAPTER 24 The Opposition to Globalization

Frankel, J. A., and D. Romer. "Does Trade Cause Growth?" *American Economic Review* 89, no. 3 (1999): 379–399.

"Indian Call Center Lands in Ohio." *Fortune*, August 6, 2007, p. 23.

Makki, Shiva S., and Agapi Somwaru. "Impact of Foreign Direct Investment and Trade on Economic Growth: Evidence from Developing Countries." *American Journal of Agricultural Economics* 86, no. 3 (2004): 795–801.

CHAPTER 25 The $750,000 Job

Congressional Budget Office. "The Pros and Cons of Pursuing Free-Trade Agreements." July 2003. (www.cbo.gov/showdoc.cfm?index=4458&sequence=0)

Greider, William. "A New Giant Sucking Sound: China Is Taking Away Mexico's Jobs as Globalization Enters a Fateful New Stage." *Nation*, December 31, 2001, p. 22.

"Stolen Jobs? Offshoring." *Economist*, December 13, 2003, p. 15.

CHAPTER 26 The Trade Deficit

Congressional Budget Office. "Causes and Consequences of the Trade Deficit: An Overview." March 2000. (www.cbo.gov/showdoc.cfm?index=1897&sequence=0)

Congressional Budget Office. "The Decline in the U.S. Current-Account Balance since 1991." August 2004. (www.cbo.gov/showdoc.cfm?index=5722&sequence=0)

Cooper, James C., and Kathleen Madigan. "The Trade Deficit May Soon Cause Less Pain: A Weaker Dollar and Stronger Global Demand Will Slow Down the Beast." *Business Week*, July 26, 2004, p. 27.

CHAPTER 27 The Value of the Dollar

Clark, Peter, et al. *Exchange Rates and Economic Fundamentals.* IMF Occasional Paper no. 115. Washington, D.C.: International Monetary Fund, 1994.

finance.yahoo.com/currency-converter?u. One of many private currency converters available online.

Grant, James. "Is the Medicine Worse than the Illness?" *Wall Street Journal*, December 20, 2008.

www.exchange-rates.org. One of many private currency converters available online.

INDEX

A
Abject poverty
decline of, 21–22
defined, 174
Adjustable-rate mortgage
(ARM), defined, 174
Adverse effects of trade
restrictions, 156–157
Adverse selection, 137–138
defined, 174
Affordability index, 74–75
Africa. *See also countries in*
income distribution in, 66
per capita income in, 24
poverty in, 22
tropical diseases in, 6
African Americans, income levels
of, 65
After-tax income for
innovators, 31
Age
influence on happiness, 41
median, 62
Aggregate demand, 129
decline in, 85–86
defined, 174
impact of economic stimulus
on, 85
tax cuts and, 114
Aging. *See also* Elderly
income inequality and, 64
rising health care costs
and, 89
Agricultural subsidies, reduction
in, 149
Ahmedabad, India. *See also*
India
textile industry in, 12–13
underground economy in, 13
Aid to Families With Dependent
Children (AFDC), 65
Algeria. *See also* Africa
capitalism in, 23
Alstom, subsidies for, 100
Alt-A mortgages, risks of, 97
American International Group
(AIG), 113, 127, 131
moral hazard problem and,
101
subsidies for, 100, 104
American Recovery and
Reinvestment Act
(ARRA) (2009), 85

Anglo Irish Bank, subsidies
for, 100
Antitrade measures, reasons
for, 153
Apparel industry, tariffs in,
157
Appropriations bills, defined,
174
Argentina
government spending in, 115
nationalization of private
pension pensions in, 115
standard of living in, 22
Asia
income distribution in, 66
industrial policy in, 102
Asset-backed security (ABS),
49, 50
defined, 174
Assets
acquisition of, 4
bank, 136
defined, 174
of elderly, 118
Fed purchase of, 131
movement of, out of
Argentina, 115
in payment of imports, 162
sell off, 155–156
following terrorist attacks,
127
Asymmetric information, 137
defined, 174
Australia
capitalism in, 22
colonial strategies in, 6
as common law nation, 4
Automobile industry. *See also*
Chrysler; Ford Motor
Company; General
Motors (GM)
adverse effects of trade
restrictions and, 156–157
bailout programs for, 113
government takeover of, 101
insourcing in, 19
limits on imports and, 153
Automobiles
Congress' attempt to pass
domestic-content bill
for, 158
constant-quality price of, 75
quality of, 75

Average income, level of, and
capitalism, 23
Average per capita incomes in
capitalist countries, 25
Average tax rate, defined, 174

B
Bailouts, 97–98, 100–105
bankruptcy and, 104
creative destruction and,
103–104
industrial policy and,
102–103, 105
moral hazard problem and,
101–102
saving of jobs and, 104
too-big-to-fail policies and,
100–101, 102, 104
Balance sheets, 51, 127
defined, 174
of Federal Reserve System,
131
Bank runs, 117, 125
defined, 135–136, 174
Bankruptcy
danger of, 170
defined, 174
of General Motors, 109
innovative destruction
and, 104
pension crisis and, 110–111
Bankruptcy Code
Chapter 9 of, 110
defined, 174
Banks
creation of Federal Reserve
System to serve as lender
of last resort, 126
defined, 175
excess reserves held by, 128
payment of interests on
reserves held by, 128
Barrett, Craig, 17
Bear Stearns, subsidies
for, 100
Beggar-thy-neighbor policies,
150–151
Behavior, effect of taxes on, 31
Bernanke, Ben, 126, 127
BMW, 20
insourcing by, 19
Boeing Corporation, 171–172
Bondholders, defined, 174